PERFORMANCE-DRIVEN THINKING

TO
EVELYN,
YOU ARE
A
PERFORMER!

B|Li

4|14

Only by taking inspired massive action will your lucky break magically appear.

**Richard Krawczyk**

As a coach, I have guided Olympic medalists, multi-millionaires, media celebrities, and other high achievers. Honestly, these people aren't fundamentally that different from anyone else—with one exception. David Hancock and Bobby Kipper have nailed exactly what that exception is—and how you can use it yourself to go, quite literally, as far as you want in this world.

**David Garfinkel**
*Author,* **Advertising Headlines That Make You Rich**

I thoroughly enjoyed reading *Performance-Driven Thinking*. In today's fast-paced world, this type of thinking will help keep you focused and aligned with your core values. It is a mindset you need to be who you truly are meant to be! I highly recommend this to anyone looking for a competitive edge.

**Ali Pervez**
www.alipervez.com *#1 bestselling marketing author*

In *Performance-Driven Thinking*, David Hancock and Bobby Kipper change the conversation about what it takes to live a fulfilled life. What makes high performers succeed while others fail? How can you duplicate their success? This book answers those questions, and more.

**Ray Edwards**
www.RayEdwards.com

Mind shifting! Bobby Kipper and David Hancock compel you to move from bystander to powerful performer faster than you think is possible. Their remarkable insights give you the top-level performance, personal excellence, leveraged efficiency, and freeing balance you deserve in your life and business. Grab this book today, because it will transform your life forever.

**Ken McArthur**

*Bestselling author of **Impact: How to Get Noticed, Motivate Millions, and Make a Difference in a Noisy World***

David Hancock and Bobby Kipper deliver an outstanding product for anybody who is looking to take their performance to a new level in any aspect of life.

*Performance-Driven Thinking* is thought provoking, sound, applicable, and inspirational. When applied, the wisdom offered in this book will propel you further than you can imagine. Time spent reading this important book is well invested.

**Bethany Marshall**
*Professional MMA fighter*

*Performance-Driven Thinking* is a refreshing look into the importance of cultivating the often-overlooked foundations for success: the right mindset, attitude, and ability to focus. The writing is clear and motivating, with plenty of concrete tips woven throughout the book. A must-read for anyone looking to level up success in their business!

**Dina Proctor**
*Bestselling author of **Madly Chasing Peace***

If performance in life and what it takes to succeed have always baffled you, this book is the key to unlock these mysteries. *Performance-Driven Thinking* will help you understand that you have everything it takes to excel both personally and professionally. I am recommending it to every member of my department, from firefighter to chief officer.

**Sharon K. Caughlin**

*Division Chief, Chesapeake Fire Department*

*Performance-Driven Thinking* clearly sets a path for everyone to get started on the performance of their dreams. David Hancock and Bobby Kipper have taken performance to a new level with this compelling book.

I highly recommend *Performance-Driven Thinking*.

**Rick Frishman**

*Founder, Planned Television Arts*

*Performance-Driven Thinking* is the required mindset for unlocking and utilizing your full potential in the twenty-first century. Kipper and Hancock have written a thoughtful, well-organized guide that provides essential advice for entrepreneurs, athletes, and anyone looking to get ahead in business and in life. It will be required reading for my athletes and clients.

**John O'Sullivan**

*Professional soccer coach*

*Author, **Changing the Game: The Parents' Guide to Raising Happy, High-Performing Athletes** and **Giving Youth Sports Back to Our Kids***

Cut to the chase and win the race. High performers David Hancock and Bobby Kipper share profound insights into the mindset of the champions. In a simple and accessible way, they help you to become laser-focused, to live the life you were born to live, and to perform on all cylinders every step of the way. If mediocrity is not your destination, you need this book.

### Sky Blossoms

*Intuitive guide and speaker*
*Author,* ***Best Thing Ever: Escape Disappointments and Drama and Let True Love Into Your Life***

*Performance-Driven Thinking* will change your world!

David Hancock and Bobby Kipper share proven strategies and give useful motivational tools page after page as they define what and who a Performance-Driven Thinker is.

My life will forever be brighter after reading this book! Why? *Performance-Driven Thinking* helped restore the needed balance in my life! It helped me understand that I am a Performance-Driven Thinker—I am the greatest performer in my life!

By taking a journey through this wonderfully written manuscript, you too will awaken, feeling a fresh new outlook on life!

### Christine Malone

*Author,* ***Christine's Kilimanjaro***

*Performance-Driven Thinking* is a wonderfully crafted book that examines how to arouse consciousness and leverage accumulated knowledge, talents, and skills into peak performances. Stories are skillfully woven throughout the book to illustrate the complexity of the issues in a simplistic way. It is a must-read book!

### Ché D. Henderson

*Principal, V2K, Inc.*
*President-Elect, Habitat for Humanity Peninsula*
*and Greater Williamsburg*

*Performance-Driven Thinking* puts you on the fast track to personal success. This information shifted my perspective on myself and my business from ordinary to extraordinary in record time!

### Robert D. Bessler

*Author,* **Expansion Mastery: The Practical Guide to Living a Fully Engaged Life**

The world is your stage. This book is an essential guide that provides practical how-to steps to succeed with *Performance-Driven Thinking*. Balance is the new lever. You were born to perform. Now is your time!

### Janet I. Mueller

*Founder of Leadership in Excellence Academy*
*Speaker, coach, and Author of* **A Champion's Guide to Thriving Beyond Breast Cancer**

David Hancock is a driven entrepreneur who has built an empire from scratch. With Bobby Kipper, David embraces the perspective for achieving your best in *Performance-Driven Thinking*. It's a must-read!

**Bryan Eaton**

*Author,* **Success Platforms**
SuccessPlatforms.com

As a fellow entrepreneur, *Performance-Driven Thinking* was a joy to read. Finally, a clear way to explain myself to those who want to know who I am, how I think, and what motivates me to do the things I do. I see Performance Driven Thinking as an excellent foundational document for the building of a performance driven culture in any organization.

**Steve W. Griffin**

*Chairman and CEO*
*CML Entertainment*

*Performance-Driven Thinking* offers a paradigm shift to change the conversation landscape about the path people should consider to achieve personal excellence. It adds a much different and thought provoking perspective for anyone to emerge into their new 'self.' Authors David Hancock and Bobby Kipper really put it out there with an 'in your face gut check' that will eliminate personal excuses for anyone who is wondering 'when is it my turn to succeed?' *Performance-Driven Thinking* can change the lens of leadership at a time when the world is wondering 'what's next for leadership?' It offers a credible answer simply from its easy to apply principles to improve capability and personal commitment that begins in the title. *Performance-Driven Thinking* will be required reading and the pre-work for our students in the years to come.

### Damian D. "Skipper" Pitts

*Founder/CEO, The Leadership Bar -*
*A Professional Development Center*

*Performance-Driven Thinking* should be prescribed to all as medicine for the mind. For, within its pages we discover the cure for the cancer called average that has ravaged our world leaving behind pandemic numbers of people who simply exist or at best endure life. Those who read *Performance-Driven Thinking* and apply what is learned will begin to enjoy the life others only dream of.

### Shonn Keels

*Pastor, Evangelist, Teacher, Entrepreneur, Best Selling Author*
*and Team Leader* TeamImpact.com

*Performance-Driven Thinking* is a must read! Whether in your personal or professional life, the message that David Hancock and Bobby Kipper convey is absolutely motivational! Life may throw you curve balls every now and again, but no matter what, YOU have what it takes to overcome and be your best. Don't waste your life in the comforts of cruise control…take charge of your life, shift into high gear, and ENJOY the ride!

**Tanesha Scott**
*General Manager, Regus Management Group*

Wow! As I read *Performance-Driven Thinking*, I was struck by the consistency of aha moments and insights - even those I knew but was appropriately reminded of in the context of this topic. It takes something powerful and emotionally charged to spark real change in once's life. Performance-Driven Thinking delivers. I'm getting ready to read it again.

**Lori Ruff**
*CEO, Integrated Alliances, The LinkedIn Diva*

Anyone can talk about performance-driven thinking. These authors actually break it down and show you how you can become a performance-driven thinker right now.

**Laura Atchison**
*Business Strategist and Best Selling Author*

The world as we know it is changing fast and as a result companies are disappearing and new companies are being created. Whether you are building a personal brand, building social proof, or whether you are an entrepreneur or business leader - understanding and putting into action the principles that David Hancock and Bobby Kipper reveal in their book *Performance-Driven Thinking* will help you distinguish what separates you from choosing to be a performer or to be simply satisfied going along for the ride.

It's undeniable, all of us have something to offer or share, whether it's knowledge, skills or abilities. David and Bobby explain that: "we were born to perform and that the world is our stage". In order to separate ourselves from the crowded and noisy market place full of competition, we need to stand out and create the performance of our lives. *Performance-Driven Thinking* should challenge you to get off the sidelines and jump into your role by putting in your best performance. Nothing will happen unless you actually do something! After reading *Performance-Driven Thinking* you can't help but feel inspired and motivated to take action. This book is a must read - Bravo David and Bobby!

**Eric V. Van Der Hope**

*International Bestselling Author of*
**Mastering Niche Marketing**

An insightful and inspiring handbook on how to carry out your life's calling with precision and excellence.

**Frank Viola**

*Author,* **God's Favorite Place on Earth,** frankviola.org

If you want to go from being a passive observer to thriving participant in your own life, read *Performance-Driven Thinking*.

**Jeff Goins**

*Author,* **The In-Between**

The real American Dream is not to get a guaranteed salary, benefits and retirement - it's to perform at such a level that rewards include financial, physical, emotional, spiritual and relational abundance. *Performance-Driven Thinking* will move you from "I can" to "I will."

**Dan Miller**

*New York Times bestselling author*
**48 Days to the Work You Love**

# PERFORMANCE-DRIVEN THINKING

Published in New York, New York, by Morgan James Publishing. Morgan James and The Entrepreneurial Publisher are trademarks of Morgan James, LLC.

www.MorganJamesPublishing.com

The Morgan James Speakers Group can bring authors to your live event. For more information or to book an event visit The Morgan James Speakers Group at

www.TheMorganJamesSpeakersGroup.com.

ISBN # 9781614486930 PB
ISBN # 9781614486947 EB
Library of Congress Control Number: 2013905770

**Cover Design by:**
Brittany Douglas
www.brittanydouglasdesign.com
brittany@brittanydouglasdesign.com

**Interior Design by:**
3 Dog Design
www.3dogdesign.net
chris@3dogdesign.net

FREE eBook edition for your existing eReader with purchase

PRINT NAME ABOVE

For more information, instructions, restrictions, and to download the BitLit app, go to **www.bitlit.ca** or use your QR Reader to scan:

In an effort to support local communities, raise awareness and funds, Morgan James Publishing donates a percentage of all book sales for the life of each book to Habitat for Humanity Peninsula and Greater Williamsburg.

Get involved today, visit
www.MorganJamesBuilds.com.

Habitat for Humanity®
Peninsula and
Greater Williamsbur
Building Partner

# PERFORMANCE-DRIVEN THINKING

A Challenging Journey That Will
Encourage You to Embrace the
Greatest Performance of Your Life

**David L. Hancock and Bobby Kipper**

NEW YORK

# To Jay Conrad Levinson (1933–2013)

There are so many places to start, so many stories to pass on. It is hard to decide where to begin. I could start with the story of how Jay convinced me to write my first book. Or the story of how we first met in person at Armand Morin's Big Seminar over six years after starting to write together. Or the story of how Jay and I sat for hours in his home talking about his journey in the desert. They are all amazing.

Jay was a phenomenal storyteller. Most great leaders are. I loved each and every one of his stories. He was entertaining, inspiring, encouraging, and of course, very educating. My favorites are the classics like the birth of the Marlboro Man and how Tabasco grew back to profitability with one amazingly simple trick. Or how he and Jeannie married on their very first date (which was the very first time they met). Like I said, they are all great stories, and I've heard them all.

But I'll start with a more personal one.

Almost exactly two years ago, while having dinner at Smokey Bones with Jeannie and Jay in Florida, Jay turned to me and said that he'd like to tell me a story. I immediately laughed and said that I've heard them all, but I could hear them all over and over again. He smiled and said that this one he could guarantee I had not heard before. "Challenge accepted," I said.

He proceeded to tell me, with his usual, carefully chosen words—with joy and purpose—that five months ago he was diagnosed with a rare form of bone marrow cancer.

He was right. I had not heard that story. My heart dropped into my stomach as I listened on.

He went on to tell me that it was incurable and untreatable, and he was given less than six months to live.

I couldn't hold back my tears. I was getting all choked up as I tried to tell him that I didn't want to hear that story. Jay comforted me as he continued. He looked at me with a big smile and told me not to be sad. He said the story has a very happy ending.

Then he went on to tell me how he's lived a full life. He's accomplished every goal he set out. He listed literally dozens of amazing moments in his life. I could barely keep up.

He then told me of how amazingly grateful he was to have me in his life. And how much fun he's having writing and publishing with me.

I lost it.

Of all the talents Jay had, and this is so true, his most endearing talent was his ability to make you feel like it was more of an honor for him to be with you than the other way around. He was a very gracious, loving man—as you can see in this short video interview from October 2008, when he ambushed my praise of him and turned it on me (http://youtu.be/ziM_gR479AY).

Let me get back to the happy ending.

Jay continued to tell me all the joys he had as our lives intersected. Then he paused, smiled even bigger, and said, "I've filled my bucket to overflowing and I'm ready to kick it!" We both laughed out loud. It was too clever of a quip not to.

We all were blessed to have him in our lives, and he defied the odds, as he always had with everything he did.

He passed at home in Jeannie's arms, early in the morning of October 10, 2013.

Join with me not in the mourning of his passing, but the joy and celebration of his life!

Jay, I will always love you, and I am eternally grateful to have had you in my life. You were, as I said before, very entertaining, inspiring, encouraging, and educating. You taught me so many things, including the importance of having balance—which is what Performance-Driven Thinking is all about.

Thank you, Jay, for including me on your journey, and being a part of mine.

*David L. Hancock*

# CONTENTS

# Acknowledgments

As we continue on our journey of performance, we realize that without the help of top performers, this dream would not have become a reality. We would sincerely like to express our great appreciation to the following individuals for their valued support and Performance-Driven attitude in helping us bring this project to completion:

Rick Frishman, *publisher*
Jim Howard, *publishing director*
Margo Toulouse, *managing editor*
Amanda Rooker, *developmental editor*
Brittany Douglas, *cover design and branding*
Chris Treccani, *interior design and layout*
Nate Razzano, *website development*
Bethany Marshal, *marketing and publicity liaison*

We would also both like to thank our families and individual friends who throughout our lives have enabled us to pursue the performance of a lifetime. Most importantly, we want to thank those who read this book and use it.

# FOREWORD

Whether you were awakened this morning by the sun streaming through your window, your phone alarm playing your favorite ringtone, the kids jumping on the bed, the dog licking at your face, or just naturally wiping the sleep from your eyes without any external prompting, odds are that if you are reading these words, you did indeed wake up!

And that, my friend, is your call to action.

You see, I believe every person on the face of the earth was created by God with unique passions, talents, skills, abilities, and personality, which, when mixed together and placed inside a physical body (which looks a lot like you!), makes them completely unique from anyone who has ever, or will ever, live. That means you are truly one of a kind!

If that's true (and I'm certain that it is), that means your unique composition qualifies you to bring value to the world in a way no one else can. Sure, others may be in similar vocations, but I guarantee that you have a special "something" that no one else has.

Remember the wind-up wristwatch? Many people have stopped wearing the old-school watch and now prefer an LED readout, while others have left their wrists naked, since their phones tell time so accurately. However, I know some people still wear these mechanical devices. I personally find wind-up watches fascinating.

Did you know that there are well over one hundred parts in a Rolex watch? Each part is essential to the form and function of the watch. Without one of these parts, the watch would fail to look like a Rolex or operate perfectly like a Rolex.

If a cog in a watch is essential for keeping perfect time, how much more essential is it that you play the role you were designed to play?

I would submit to you that playing your role (as your authentic self) is so important that not to do so would be to do a disservice to the world around you. Yes, you are that important!

While in the context of acting, performance is clearly about being someone else, that's not the kind of performing this book is about.

Performance is not about being anything and anyone other than who you are. It's also not about meeting someone else's standards. It's about gratefully welcoming the new day and the opportunities it provides to show up and be the best you possible. It's an invitation to live out your God-given uniqueness in a way that positively impacts the lives of others.

When we are living from our true selves and seeking to bring value to the lives of others, we don't have to worry about what's in it for ourselves. When we make it our aim to "deliver the goods" through our relationships, words, and actions, we can be sure that we have done the best we can do, even if imperfectly. And when we can look back at the day, knowing we've done the best we can, that's where we find true satisfaction in our work.

So what causes one person to perform and another to wave the white flag? What practical steps can you take to sharpen your mindset and perform more effectively?

The book you are holding is important. Bobby Kipper and David Hancock have thoroughly researched Performance-Driven Thinking, and they have demonstrated the principles they teach by stepping up and writing this book. It is a manifestation of the very mindset they hope to pass on to you.

Count yourself fortunate if you are reading these words. Not everyone had the same opportunity to welcome this new day. That means you've got work to do. It's time to show up and shine. The world is waiting for you.

Joel Comm
*New York Times* bestselling author
www.JoelComm.com

# CHAPTER 1:

## You Were Born to Perform

You have waited for months to see your favorite band. The tickets sold out quickly, but you were fortunate enough to land a couple. You grab your favorite partner and head out for a nice dinner before the show. After dropping just over fifty dollars for a great meal, including drinks, you head to the sold-out concert venue. You arrive in heavy traffic and find your seats. After the opening band plays, there is a brief intermission and the lights go out. You are psyched as you wait for the main act. The stage is set, the moment has arrived, and excitement fills the air. The long-awaited band takes the stage, the lights flash on—yet there is a noticeable silence. The band is just standing there, instruments in hand, completely still and silent. The crowd gets restless and begins to clap in sync. Where is the music? Why isn't the group performing? *What's going on?*

After a period of time, the band leaves the stage and the house lights come on. The announcer lets the crowd know that the band has decided not to play tonight. *How could that happen?*

It happens every day all over the world. Since the day you were born, the stage for you to perform has been set. It begins when we are infants and continues on throughout our lives. Our first steps are celebrated. Our first words are captured and applauded. Your first day of school is a milestone. The day you graduate from high school is recorded and remembered. But what makes these moments special is not just about that present achievement, as important as it is. It's the fact that this achievement marks the threshold of an even bigger opportunity. At each new juncture, you apply what you learn and take the next step. You didn't learn to walk to stop short of learning to run. You didn't learn to add to stop short of learning to multiply. The key moments in our lives are all about learning how to perform—and going on to perform on a bigger stage.

Your knowledge, skills, and abilities were no accidents. And your God-given talents were not intended to be wasted. If we look around our world today, we could all name individuals who could have made a huge difference in life if they would have performed to their abilities. People who had the talent and opportunity but just would not take the next step toward performance.

So why *do* some people take the stage in life, while others hesitate? That is the magic question that faces our entire society. Parents wonder why some children perform and others hold back. Educators are equally perplexed, spending countless hours (and dollars) trying to motivate performance in students. And despite the myriad of books and systems guaranteeing better performance and productivity, most businesses still struggle to find the right formula that works long term. While most of our programming and efforts in the past several years have focused on group or team performance, one central issue still remains. We cannot escape the fact that performance (or the lack thereof) is fundamentally an individual decision.

Look around and answer this question: if the people within your scope of influence fail to perform, whose fault is it? While you can encourage performance as a leader, you cannot perform for others. Just as you were born to perform, so were they. We are all born with some level of opportunity. Some were born with certain obstacles, but look at the countless people in our society who have overcome obstacles such as disease and birth defects to become champions. War-battered heroes have returned to our society and have become inspirational leaders. Cancer survivors have battled their disease and have pushed onward. Victims of crime and disorder in our society have started national efforts to fight for the rights of others who have faced injustice.

If our bodies were programmed to perform, everyone would automatically perform to the limit of their ability. But we know that's not the case. Some people wait for their ship to come in; others swim out to it. Some people wait for the right time; others say there is no time like today. Some people wait for the right circumstances; others create their own circumstances regardless of ability, heredity, or opportunity.

So again, what separates those who choose to perform and those who become idle in their efforts?

This question has perplexed both David and I (Bobby) throughout our years in leadership in both the public and private sectors.

I first noticed performance issues in the workplace when I began my career in law enforcement at the young age of 20. Since the third grade, I had wanted to be a police officer. I made it my goal to proudly wear the badge and gun in an effort to change society. I can recall working hard as a detective to clear cases. At the same time, other investigators displayed an attitude of coasting along when it came to their caseload. Obviously there was a significant difference in the performance of those who worked hard and those who just coasted along.

But the surprising aspect, which was consistent throughout all my years working in the police department and in local government, was that everyone received the same yearly raise whether they produced effort or not. Non-performers received the same incremental increase in pay as performers. This was my first introduction to what I learned later was a status-quo attitude toward performance and overall effort. As a person who is driven by performance, this both perplexed and disappointed me. We will reflect more on this issue in chapters 4 and 6, where we discuss workplace performance.

In addition to the workplace, I also noticed performance issues in the area of organized athletics. For over thirty years I have had the honor and enjoyment of being involved in the world of sports as a high school official, prep school coach, and Little League coach. As a top-level high school basketball official, I had the opportunity to be involved in a number of games where it was evident that players were giving their very best effort in pursuing their goals of winning the contest. But surprisingly, I can also recall a number of games where players appeared to be simply going through motions of participating, acting as if losing was no big deal.

As a coach at the youth sports and prep-school level, I have coached players with little ability, as well as those with excellent athletic skills. I have always been amazed at the varying degrees of attitude toward performance among both talented and less-talented athletes alike. At times it seemed that a number of players with natural God-given talents did not possess that so-called "killer instinct," while many who struggled with their abilities possessed a truly performance-driven attitude and superior work ethic.

Suffice to say, I have been perplexed about this question of why some individuals are driven to perform while others appear to be going along for the ride. But all of my thoughts and questions in this area came to a head during my oldest daughter's high school basketball game several years ago. During the second half of the game, an errant pass between players was heading out of bounds when my daughter, Jolie, dove after the loose ball to save it for her team. After she made the play that every dad and coach would marvel at, I was approached by one of the most successful men I knew, also attending the game, who posed an interesting question. He asked, "What causes a kid to do that?" I looked at this gentleman with a puzzled look and responded, "I'm not sure I can answer that."

As her dad, of course, I wanted to take credit for her sudden outburst of amazing performance. But I quickly realized that what Jolie displayed was an individual quality and not something I could just give her. She was driven to go after the ball while others stood and watched the play. You see, others could have put forth the same effort, but something made her want it more. At that moment, I realized that there had to be a specific thought process that defines our inner initiative, or the lack thereof. It has to be more than instinct; it has to be more than heredity.

That was when David Hancock and I began our conversations about what really drives performance. David is an entrepreneur and founder of Morgan James Publishing, as well as my friend, colleague, and business coach, so I had already noticed he had certain qualities that seemed to result in consistent performance and success. For example, I had noticed that he invested heavily in his employees who showed a natural drive to perform, because helping them succeed helped his business succeed. Being the inquisitive guy I am, I asked him many more questions about why he made the kinds of decisions he did, which began a deeper discussion about performance in general.

Together David and I began to examine the characteristics of individuals who perform at the highest level despite massive obstacles, and to seek workable solutions for those who, for some reason or another, simply don't step up to the stage.

We realized that almost everyone has the desire to perform and may even know that they were born to perform. But that's not enough. There has to be a conscious *decision* to perform. Even the best-trained athletes have to have the thought that translates to the will to perform. How many times have you heard the statement "They just didn't show up tonight" when describing a team that suffered a huge loss? Does this mean that they were not physically present? Of course not. They were there in body, but not in thought. They did not leave behind their ability to perform; they left behind their will to perform. Sports stars, musicians, great actors, and other successful people do not perform by accident. Inevitably they have the stamina of thought *and* will to push through the tough process that eventually will lead them to peak performance on the world's biggest stages, whatever their fields may be. It comes down to their ability to know what they want and to have the mental strength to go for it.

So we realized that performance didn't depend solely on the desire to succeed, and it didn't solely depend on the effort or will to succeed. The two needed to be connected through a particular thought process. We have defined this process as Performance-Driven Thinking, and we think it could change your life!

Here is our definition of Performance-Driven Thinking:

---

### PERFORMANCE-DRIVEN THINKING:
*The thought process that connects the **desire** to perform with the **will** to perform a specific task or goal.*

**DESIRE:** *To long or hope for something you want.*

**WILL:** *To decide, attempt, or bring desire to action.*

---

This definition is based not merely on research but on reality. You can't begin to perform until you make a conscious decision to do so. But our purpose in writing this book goes beyond simply defining Performance-Driven Thinking. It truly is our desire to bring it out in you! We don't want you to waste another day without stepping up to the plate. We don't want you to continue to go through life wondering what could have been if you had only taken that next step. No matter how big or small, your next step could be the one that changes your life.

If we want to raise the level of performance in our people and ourselves, we need more than simply coaching or encouragement. We need to understand what is missing in our thinking so we can plug in what is needed. That's exactly what you will learn in this book.

Because David and I come at Performance-Driven Thinking from different perspectives, we thought it best to address it separately from our own unique vantage points. In the main text of each chapter, I will cover Performance-Driven Thinking from a more practical, on-the-ground perspective, based on my years of experience as a coach and public servant in the police force. In the sidebars, David will cover Performance-Driven Thinking from a visionary and business strategy perspective, based on his years as a successful entrepreneur and business owner. Taken together, we believe you'll get a fuller picture of what Performance-Driven Thinking is all about, no matter what context you find yourself in—and how to start using it in your own life, beginning now.

# Performance-Driven Thinking: The Goal Is the Journey

First of all, congratulations on even considering becoming a Performance-Driven Thinker in a new, rapidly changing world. It's challenging, but you're in for a lot of fun. Work? Of course, lots of work, but fun too. Lots of fun, if you do it right.

The first thing you'll notice about being a Performance-Driven Thinker is that your goals will be different from the old-fashioned goals of a non-Performance-Driven Thinker. If you're an entrepreneur or a business owner, for example, a Performance-Driven Enterprise is flexible, innovative, unconventional, low in overhead costs, dependent, interactive, generous, enjoyable, and profitable. The goal of the enterprise is to stay that way.

Look at the entrepreneurs all around you. If you can't see many, it's because they are not Performance-Driven Thinkers. Instead they're buried in work, rarely coming up for the fresh air of free time. When you learn to truly perform, you become far more efficient and effective. In fact, the goals of Performance-Driven Thinkers allow them the freedom to pursue interests beyond work—while amassing an income beyond that of their workaholic ancestors.

You can always tell Performance-Driven Thinkers by their goals. They are not as money minded as the entrepreneurs who came before them. They seem to be happier with the work that they're doing and appear to care like crazy about satisfying the needs of their customers. You've never seen follow-up done the way these people do it. They stay in touch constantly with their customers. It's not as if they are working at their business, but rather demonstrating passion for their work. Their goal is to express that passion with excellence and transform it into profits.

Not surprisingly, Performance-Driven Thinkers achieve their goals on a daily basis. Their long-term goals are lofty. Those goals exist in the future. Their short-term goals are even loftier. Those exist in the present, for that is the domain of the Performance-Driven Thinker. That is where her goals are to be found in abundance.

Your ability to plan for the future and learn from the past will determine your level of comfort in the present, in the here and now. Being a Performance-Driven Thinker means realizing that these can be the good old days and that you don't have to wait for the joy that comes with success. It's there in front of you, in the present moment.

Wake up from the Old American Dream and realize that it has changed for the better—the New American Dream is more achievable, more enjoyable, and much healthier than the old one.

Although at this moment you may find the New American Dream unconventional, as all Performance-Driven endeavors are, you'll soon see that it will come to be the mainstream American Dream, because it is achievable and brings increased benefits. Most of us can dream it and then delight in making it come true.

Originally, the dream meant having enough food and protection from the weather. Cave dwellers dreamt of hunting enough game or gathering an abundance of nuts and berries. That dream has changed, replaced by the hope of earning enough money to feed a hungry family. The Industrial Revolution took care of that and eventually gave birth to the American Dream: a house, a job, and financial security.

Entrepreneurs of the twentieth century were motivated by a slightly different version of the American Dream. In place of a house, a job, and financial security, they sought fortune, security, expansion, and power. But that journey was characterized by workaholism, sacrifice, and greed.

The entrepreneur of the future will need to be a Performance-Driven Thinker—one who thrives on the non-traditional, does the unconventional if the conventional is nonsensical, and knows that working in the new millennium requires rethinking the nature of being a successful entrepreneur.

The performance goals of the twentieth-century entrepreneur were simple—securing a job, a family, a home. The goals of the Performance-Driven Thinker are considerably loftier than those of the past: attaining work that is satisfying, enough money to enjoy freedom from worry about it, health good enough to take for granted, a family or bonding with others in which you can give and receive love and support, fun that does not have to be pursued but exists in daily living, and the longevity to appreciate with wisdom that which you and those you love have achieved.

Balance will be the new dream. Performance-Driven Thinkers who go about creating a profit-producing enterprise will begin with balance, actually starting with work that makes them happy, the goal of all Performance-Driven dreams. Once that has been attained, Performance-Driven Thinkers will be able to pursue their other goals: making money, enjoying free time, maintaining health, and having fun.

Most important, as I (David) hope you realize, the goal of the Performance-Driven Thinker is the journey itself.

So we take on this journey of performance. Our goal is not to measure knowledge, skills, and ability, but to wake up and motivate the conscious desire to perform—and connect it to the will to perform. Many people are asleep at the wheel in their personal and professional lives. They fail to perform, so they fail to make a difference—not simply because they don't want to, but because they have reached a point where staying idle is easier. Is that person you? Is that person in your family, perhaps one of your children? Is that person someone who works with you or for you?

You're going to have a chance to diagnose whether you are a bystander or a performer in chapter 10, after you've had a chance to learn more about what Performance-Driven Thinking really entails. But whether you're already a performer, a bystander, or somewhere in between, this process is not about finger pointing. It is about moving beyond where you are and reaching out to where you could be. Think what the world would be like if everyone stepped up to the stage and performed. What would happen in our homes, businesses, and communities?

Performance-Driven Thinking is the first step. Beginning this journey is a personal choice—no one can make you perform except you. And Performance-Driven Thinking begins with the clear understanding that we were born to perform. The world is our stage. Opportunities already surround us that will allow us to step up and take part in the performance of our lives.

Don't miss out on the greatest opportunity that you will ever have. Your lights will only burn for the season of your life. It's never too late to take the stage. Step up and enjoy the ride: your audience is waiting. *You were born to perform!*

**"The difference between a successful person and others is not a lack of strength, not a lack of knowledge, but rather a lack of will."**

**Vince Lombardi**

# CHAPTER 2:

# When Everybody Gets a Trophy:

## Obstacles to Performance-Driven Thinking

Even though our journey toward performance is based on our individual thoughts and actions, we all have to face some outward obstacles. One of the biggest, in my opinion, is the cultural mindset of entitlement.

A few years ago I had the opportunity to coach my son's Little League baseball team. It was an exciting and challenging experience. I really enjoyed teaching the kids to improve their game in both hitting and fielding. The trouble was that we did not do either very well. At the end of the season, we had managed only to win three games in an eleven-game season. A few days before our last game, I was riding in the car with my son when he asked an interesting question. "So Dad, when do we get our trophies?"

I must admit I was dismayed that Andrew felt he and his fellow teammates deserved trophies for a losing season. My curiosity took over, and I asked him, "Why do you think you and the team deserve to get a trophy?" His answer actually shocked me: "Dad, everybody gets a trophy."

I felt saddened that my son, at age ten, had been conditioned to believe that everybody deserves to reap rewards even when their performance level does not merit it. Then it occurred to me that this mindset is not just true of our kids; it has become true of who we are as a nation.

Today, our children become indoctrinated with this entitlement mindset at an early age, often with youth sports. Years ago we stopped declaring winners and losers, and now everybody gets a trophy. Children who have little or no skill level are decorated for mere participation. These same groups of children then show up at the doors of our educational institutions and act oppressed when they discover that grades must be earned and are awarded based on whether a student performs according to an objective standard. But wait: many school districts have now lowered the bar on the grading scale. In some cases, children are passed on to a higher grade without earning it. In many cases when children fail to perform, we overly blame the educator and fail to appropriately blame the individual student.

Thus some children are set up for failure from the start. They are rewarded in sports for their presence, not performance. They move on in school and are passed on to a higher grade through presence, not performance. And then they show up at work and have a problem with understanding a merit pay system, or worse, they enter the workforce without a solid work ethic.

This sense of entitlement happens "when everybody gets a trophy," whether it's in sports or in school or at work. It happens when rewards are not earned; they are expected. This style of thinking inhibits personal performance and can become very contagious in the absence of clear-cut expectations. In fact, entitlement thinking, and those who seek and practice it, destroys the very heart of performance.

The important issue to grasp is that while performance is an individual choice, entitlement is an easy hiding place, especially in group settings such as offices of organizations with a number of employees. And once this sense of entitlement starts, it acts as a quick-spreading disease. What motivates an individual's work ethic outside of the will to perform? Regardless of your upbringing or other developmental circumstances, performance still comes down to a choice. That same choice drives the masses to entitlement.

Imagine being invited to a dinner that will feature an award ceremony. After a nice meal, the leader of the group stands in front of the crowd and calls you up to present you with a performance award. When you receive the award, you see that there is one major problem: it has someone else's name on it. Clearly there has been a mistake, and you have not actually won an award. The award was intended for someone else. Would you accept the award, even though someone else clearly earned it?

Most people would say no. But this same scenario takes place every day in America, where people who don't perform truly believe they should be rewarded in the same way as those who do. There are people on the playing field of life who forgo the pride of performance and embrace the comfort of entitlement. That's right: performance brings out pride. Entitlement brings out complaints. Performers are never satisfied, but they don't complain. Entitlement seekers are satisfied (with not performing), but they still complain. Performers want to grow. Entitlement seekers want to maintain the status quo with their current rewards. Performers let their actions speak. Entitlement seekers speak to cover up their actions. Performers embrace challenges. Entitlement seekers ignore challenges.

The important question is: would you rather be a performer, or an entitlement seeker? Would your company rather hire performers, or entitlement seekers?

Here's the bigger question: How can you ensure that you are a performer? And how can your organization identify and reward performers?

We're going to help you answer these questions in much more detail in the following chapters. But for now, one easy way to know is that performers will seek out spoken or unspoken expectations. So if you want to know what's expected to succeed, you are on your way to Performance-Driven Thinking. If your organization has clear expectations of your employees, then you are on your way to encouraging performance as an organization.

# Ten Dirty Lies You Have Known and Loved

As we said in the last chapter, the goal of the Performance-Driven Thinker is the journey itself.

But this has not been the way with most entrepreneurs, even if they value this way of thinking. Why?

In addition to our love affair with entitlement, at least ten additional reasons explain this situation. We've been led down ten garden paths that lead to the economic and social swamp in which we find ourselves mired at the moment. The time has come for us to make ten U-turns. Forget what the signs say—and what your parents and teachers said about those supposedly one-way streets. U-turns are highly recommended for any traveler who wants to reach the destination, not to mention thoroughly enjoy the journey.

If you cease believing in these ten dirty lies, you'll be well on your way to dreamland. Amending your beliefs begins with recognizing the myths you subscribe to. Once you do that, I doubt that you'll need me to puncture the myths for you. No doubt you'll see the bright light illuminating the truth. Here are the lies you must *stop believing.*

**1. Time is money.** This is a blatant untruth made up by those who are on hourly wages, frequently minimum wage. Time is far more valuable than money. If you run out of money, there are many ways to get more. If you run out of time, you can't get more.

**2. Owning a business means workaholism.** People who are workaholics prefer work to every other activity, including spending time with friends, family, and interests beyond work. Workaholism is the direct result of poor planning. Owning a business should not mean that a business owns you.

**3. Marketing is expensive.** Actually, bad marketing is expensive and good marketing is inexpensive. Performance-Driven Thinkers wouldn't think of using expensive marketing, but they know they must get the word out about their business, so they utilize inexpensive marketing with skill and fervor using time, energy, imagination, and information instead of the brute force of mega-bucks.

**4. Big corporations are like wombs.** Big corporations used to be like wombs, but these days many are like tombs. They employee the living dead who work with devotion, yet will be squeezed out kicking and screaming because of merging, downsizing, cost-cutting, restructuring, and bankruptcy. If you want a corporation that functions like a womb, form it yourself.

5. Youth is better than age. People who believe this one are usually young. Getting old means trading in some abilities to acquire others. It means losing some body power, but gaining mind power, and not making the same mistake twice, or even

once. It also helps you understand yourself and realize what wisdom really is.

**6. You need a job.** You need work, no doubt about it. And a job, structured by someone other than yourself, is one form of work. The truth for most people is that you do not need a standard nine-to-five job working for someone other than yourself—and if you do, expect to pay a high price in abdicating your freedom and the discovery of your unique essence. But you do need to work. Work should help you enjoy your freedom and discover your essential talents. Performance-Driven Thinkers love their work, but they're usually jobless. They establish the structure of their work rather than rely on an employer.

**7. Heaven is in the afterlife.** Heaven is here and heaven is now, if you know where to look for it. Living your life as though heaven existed somewhere else and in some other time means missing the point of your life. Instead, live this life so that the heaven that follows has a lot to live up to.

**8. The purpose of education is to teach facts.** The real purpose of education is to teach people to love learning. The more you love learning, the better informed you'll be throughout your life. Constant learning will always be your ally. Performance-Driven Thinkers realize that times are always changing and that growing up is a process that should never end.

**9. Retirement is a good thing.** Pay close attention here: retirement can be fatal. It often leads to inactivity, which can lead to an early demise. If you desire longevity, don't consider total retirement. People who completely retire shut down vital systems in their hearts, minds, souls, and spirits. It's okay to cut down on your own workload, even cut down drastically, but never eliminate it. Don't forget that the way of the Performance-Driven Thinker is characterized by balance. Retirement can lead to imbalance, not to mention boredom.

**10. If you want it done right, do it yourself.** This is the battle cry of the terminal workaholic. The battle cry of the Performance-Driven Thinker is, "Don't do anything you can properly delegate." It is usually unwise to think nobody can do things right except you. Such a mindset means you lack the ability to train or to link with others, mandatory skills in today's economy.

Once you're free of the shackles of these ten lies, you can focus on your goals, one key to succeeding as a Performance-Driven Thinker. (See chapter 10 for a list of good goals, or signposts, for Performance-Driven Thinkers.) To reach your goals, you must not only be aware of them, but also acknowledge that goals change.

One more thing. While striving for your goals, you will form a friendship with an ugly ally, one you'll try to avoid. As an entrepreneur who takes risks, you will not be able to avoid it forever. This ally is called failure. Get to know it—for if you take pains to eliminate it entirely, you will live a boring life indeed.

Failure is part of the deal when you're a Performance-Driven Thinker. I have failed so many times, failure grins in recognition when it sees me. Just because failure is instructive and has a lesson neatly tucked into it doesn't mean it's any fun. But Performance-Driven Thinkers learn to construct safety nets in the form of alternative sources of income, so failure isn't the ogre it used to be.

Performance-Driven Thinkers in the coming century will not have a single career like Grandpa (or maybe even Mom) did. In *Search of Excellence* author Tom Peters said, "I believe, along with British management guru Charles Handy, that a 'career' tomorrow will most likely consist of a dozen jobs on and off payrolls of large and small firms in two or three industries."

The way of the Performance-Driven Thinker generates several streams of income to support his life. If one stream dries up, financial nourishment comes from another stream. No single stream may produce enough income, but together they create a mighty river. This enables the Performance-Driven Thinker to tap several of his or her abilities.

To thoroughly examine this trait of entitlement, one would have to look beyond the typical criteria of knowledge, skills, and abilities, and move to the bottom line of personal output. Millions of people invest a tremendous amount of time, money, and energy to gain knowledge, but they never take steps to use what they know. Millions of people possess a high level of skill in particular areas, but they never use that skill. And millions of people have a tremendous ability to perform, but they never take the stage. Some would say that these people are lazy, and they just don't care.

We believe there is another reason behind many people's lack of performance that is cultural rather than individual, and that's the culture of entitlement. America's sense of entitlement impacts many. Its effects are felt in education, sports, and businesses. People from all walks of life would rather put their life in neutral and not step on the gas. As we drive down life's highway, we often see road signs that say, "Slower vehicles stay right." Is your life that slower vehicle? Would you like to finally enter the passing lane of life? What is holding you back from pushing your gas pedal? Entitlement dwellers love the slow lane of life, while performers embrace the passing lane.

In this culture of entitlement, being Performance Driven is not easy. Others around you may be stuck in the comfort zone of accepting trophies they did not earn. People you work with may be okay with status quo thinking.

The stage of life demands better than entitlement thinking; it demands performance. More importantly, you *deserve* better than entitlement thinking!

### FIVE KEYS TO OVERCOME ENTITLEMENT THINKING

1. Understand your personal and professional performance expectations.

2. Go beyond what's expected in your role.

3. Resist following the crowd to "entitlement."

4. Concentrate on your performance and not the performance of others.

5. Use your knowledge, skills, and abilities to the maximum.

**"Never mistake activity for achievement."**

**John Wooden**

# CHAPTER 3:

# Attitude:

## The Foundation of Performance-Driven Thinking

As we said in chapter 1, the magic question that looms large in our lives and in our society is "How do you become a Performance-Driven Thinker?" When David and I (Bobby) first approached this question, we began with the process of asking ourselves a question: What is the definition of Performance-Driven Thinking? We searched for a way to go beyond the obvious notion of "just putting performance first," because that is too simplistic. To "Just Do It," as Nike has stated over the years, assumes that people understand *how* to just perform. Again, if it were that easy, we would all just do it without thought or reservation.

A few years ago, I was asked to take on the role of coaching a group of middle school teens at a local college prep school. These kids, many of whom came from very affluent backgrounds, all appeared to be bright. They gathered together to take on the title of basketball players and represent their school in their local independent school conference.

Our first meeting was interesting. I told the teens what I expected of them as a coach. I was taken aback at the somber attitude these young men were displaying in what should have been an exciting time. So I stopped my comments and asked a simple question. "How many of you guys really want to be here?" A couple of hands were raised. I was amazed. Wow! It was the start of the season, and they couldn't care less. So I stepped back and inquired about their attitudes. One young man raised his hand and said, "Coach, last year we were 0 and 14." Apparently the basketball program had not won a game in years.

I was stunned at this "defeatist attitude" at the start of the season. I immediately threw out basketballs and said, "Let's have fun." Most of these kids were tall, some were quick, and our first practice went well. Before the kids left that day, I called the team together and declared, "I don't know what else is going to happen this year, but one thing I do know—we will not be 0 and 14." I also told them, "I do not embrace defeat, and neither will you."

These kids hadn't been winning because they mentally felt that they could not win. It had nothing to do with talent. It had everything to do with their mental approach. Several of these players attended top-notch summer basketball camps, only to be defeated within themselves on the road to performance. Physically, they embraced performance. Mentally, they could not grasp it.

The good news is that these kids came together and had a very successful season. We ended up 9 and 3, and we came in third place in the conference. But I had to ask myself, how did these young men get to the point of mentally throwing in the towel before the season even started? More importantly, what turned it around? Then I broadened the question: How about in life? Or in business? Is this mental abandonment of performance simply an athletic issue? No, it's a personal issue, and it does not start on the ball field or court. It starts within each of us. My years spent in sports and in business had convinced me that many individuals are just like these young teens. The foundation of our performance in any context comes down to the price we are willing to pay to get there.

Many systems, from athletic competitions to employee evaluations, tend to put the cart before the horse. All of these systems are based on the idea that individuals only need knowledge, skills, abilities, and opportunities to perform. But if performance was simply based on strength, talent, or IQ alone, the team with the strongest players would always win. And the business that hires the brightest people would have instant success.

The simple phenomenon of "underdog winning" destroys this logic. Sometimes the biggest, the best, and the most talented do not come out on top. Sports teams that spend millions have lost to teams with a minimal payroll. Top-25 teams have been knocked out by unranked teams. No-name start-up companies have overwhelmed the market, and handicapped individuals have succeeded in achieving goals greater than life itself.

So what gives? What connects the dots of ability and performance? In particular, what connects the underdog, mistreated and beaten down, to winning or succeeding? Performance-Driven Thinking, that's what. As we said in chapter 1, Performance-Driven Thinking is the thought process that connects the desire to perform with the will to perform a specified task or goal.

Performance comes down to connecting *desire* with the *will* to act in order to achieve. Frankly, people desire a lot of things in life, but many refuse to take action on those desires. Take the issue of losing weight. Many people have a desire to lose excess weight, but how many will carry out the necessary action to actually experience results? In business, most people want to be successful and get to the top of their pay grade. But how many are willing to put the time in to develop the skills necessary to move to the desired level? To put it in stronger terms, most people desire to win and to be successful. But many fail to connect their desire to the *will* to get the desired results. Performance-Driven Thinking is established when our wants in life are directly connected to our actions to achieve. Simply wanting without action is a simple wish that is unlikely to become reality.

Think of performance as a train, as illustrated above. The cars on this train represent your desires. You really want them to move forward down the track. The engine is the will. Without the will, the cars remain still. Imagine train cars without an engine, or a horse-drawn carriage without the horses. That's what it's like for many who have desire without the will to act. As we say in the sports world, talking about winning is the easy part. Finding a way to win is another story. It comes down to connecting your personal and professional wants with the personal and professional actions to get there.

Sometimes we have the very best intentions to perform, but we just can't seem to break out of that slump called "ordinary life." While many books and articles have been written about what causes us to hesitate to move forward, based on our years of research regarding performance, there are specific forces that can get in the way of connecting your desire with your will to act, and thus prevent you from reaching your dreams. Some of these you already know about, and some you don't. But if we were participating in a sporting event, we would try to find out what would keep us from winning, right? Obviously the first obstacle would be our "opponent."

The same is true for Performance-Driven Thinking. What is opposing your performance in both your personal and professional life? What is keeping you from connecting your desire to perform with your will to perform? Just as teams prepare for what they are going to face on the playing field, the following three steps will help you do the same on the "playing field of life."

## 1. Identify Your Opponent

Identifying your opponent is the first step to defeating that opponent. Have you ever talked to a friend or family member who, when something doesn't go the way they expect, responds, "I don't know what's wrong. I just know I can't do it." This state of confusion is like operating in life with zero gravity. They are just floating along, unable to move forward on their own terms. Identifying what opposes you is tied directly to the *will* to perform. We all recognize that in life and in business we will face opposition. So what are your opponents? Here is a list of common attitudes and actions that tend to throw us off our game.

- Lack of desire: not defining what we want

- Lack of will: not being willing to act on our desires

- Fear of failure: the belief we won't achieve what we want

- Past history: issues from our past we are still dealing with

- Lack of knowledge, skills, and abilities

- Lack of time or time-management skills

- Lack of resources

As you move forward today, take time to identify what stands in your way.

## 2. Prepare for Your Opponent

Now that you have identified what is stopping you, let's prepare to deal with it. Dig down deep to find the feeling inside that is shouting, "I know I can do this!" Years ago I worked on a White House initiative for former First Lady Laura Bush, entitled "Helping America's Youth." I can remember the phone call asking me to be a keynote presenter at the conference that was to take place at Howard University in Washington, DC. We had to be a part of a rigid dress rehearsal the night before, as each of us had to practice word for word what we would say. I can recall thinking that this would be the biggest speech of my life, and the dress rehearsal went a long way in preparing me to face and deal with my fears. Due to this practice and preparation, I was able to deliver the speech without issue.

Any worthy performance in life is worth preparing for. Just like a team practices to face its next opponent, so should you. Take the necessary time required to overcome your obstacles to performance. Walk yourself through the situation mentally to help you develop the confidence you need. Beating the odds takes more than desire. It takes action—in the form of preparation.

## 3. Expect to Win

Years ago, my daughter Jolie was playing varsity volleyball for the school she was attending. I did not know much about the rules of volleyball, but I knew it was frustrating watching players just standing around as the ball landed in front of them. After watching this lack of performance long enough, I asked Jolie about some players and their lack of effort. She told me that most of her teammates were expressing the feeling of defeat before they even took the court, reminding themselves of how in previous years they had been beat by the team they were about to face.

Many people wake up in the morning believing that their efforts will not be good enough. They hold back because they just think they won't come out ahead. Many will say, "It doesn't matter how hard I try; I won't make it." Personal doubt puts us on the path to giving up or giving in. Your top performance can't happen without a firm expectation that you are going to win, and win big!

No one ever said that every performance in life would be easy. What we do know is the steps above will certainly lighten your load and mark the pathway toward your goal to perform.

Several years ago I started a national nonprofit to prevent violence in America. I quickly learned that I had to overcome my fear of asking for financial support. I had several mental opponents that were blocking my road to success in the area of fundraising. First, I was raised without a lot of financial means. My family was materially poor but emotionally wealthy. Second, in my first career in law enforcement, we were conditioned not to ask for anything. Our role was to serve and protect. Lastly, I had a fear of rejection. I was shy about putting my hand out for donations because I was afraid it would come back empty. I knew in order for my nonprofit to make it, I had to perform in this area that made me feel uncomfortable. Fortunately David, as my business coach, convinced me that if I don't ask, I won't get. Corporate fundraising coach Roberto Candelaria gave me the skills and direction I needed. And my good friend and respected NBA basketball official, Tony Brothers, coached me into believing that people respected me and my mission, and they would support it.

So my performance was not automatic. I had to prepare for it. In a four-month period I was able to raise over $60,000 to help the nonprofit. All of these individuals were right. I could erase my doubts and move to performance, but only through preparation and believing I could do it.

What opposes you? How can you work through it? When you can identify what opposes you, prepare to deal with it, and expect to overcome it, you will be on your way to true Performance-Driven-Thinking.

# Ten Key Attitudes of Performance-Driven Thinkers

One of the most pleasurable, yet difficult, tasks for a Performance-Driven Thinker to achieve and maintain is living in the moment. You've got to begin that task right now, as you read this book, if you're to become a Performance-Driven Thinker! To do so, you'll have to let go of your old notions of work and leisure. It will mean dismantling those compartments into which you, or more likely, your great-grandparents, have divided your life.

In doing this, you'll free yourself to do things that matter to you. If you want to spend more time with your family, you'll be able to. One of the greatest rewards of being a Performance-Driven Thinker in the future will be the chance for people to recognize the pure nobility of work when it is pursued with joy rather than obligation. But work of the future will not be an obsession as it is right now. It will be part of a well-balanced existence. You will have many, better things to do than work. Oscar Wilde once said: "Work is the refuge of people who have nothing better to do."

Now, Performance-Driven Thinkers are stepping back a few paces and seeing that work is not the entire picture. Other parts of that picture include: recreation, friends, family, faith, health, location, education, travel, and free time. Have I left anything out? Probably. It's a big and beautiful picture. These are the rewards of living. The rewards should not be reserved for your retirement, because Performance-Driven Thinkers never completely retire from work. They may cut back, but they're having too much of a blast to retire. As Performance-Driven Thinkers, they want to use their longevity for meeting and savoring the elixir of surmounting new challenges as times, technology, and they themselves undergo staggering changes. As much as they feel passion for their work, Performance-Driven Thinkers never allow it to erode the other joys of living. The elixir recipe calls for enjoying life while earning a living.

In order to integrate your business with your life, exactly what do you need? You must have ten attitudes and ten pieces of real equipment. These are the ten attitudes:

1. Organization

2. Determination

3. Discipline

4. Passion

5. Love of life

6. Optimism

7. Flexibility

8. Honesty

9. Self-esteem

10. Generosity

Armed with these attitudes, you will be primed for success.

Why be defeated? It all comes down to your attitude. Start connecting what you want with action steps to achieve it! That is Performance-Driven Thinking!

**"I failed over and over in life and that's why I succeeded."**

**Michael Jordan**

# CHAPTER 4:

## *Performance-Driven Thinking in Your Personal Life*

In the first chapter, we said that you were born to perform. Most of us think that performance has to do with activities with clear external standards, such as sports, education, and employment. But in order for Performance-Driven Thinking to become a reality in our lives, it must begin within us at a personal level. In fact, personal Performance-Driven Thinking can be an even greater challenge, because there are no easy external standards to measure our performance. Personal Performance-Driven Thinking requires us to measure our personal growth and success ratio according to our own internal standards.

We all have personal areas in our lives that are critically important to each of us. They include 1) personal health, 2) personal goals, 3) personal relationships, and 4) personal finance.

## Personal Health

Performance-Driven Thinking relates to your health just as much as it relates to your professional life. Our personal health depends greatly on our personal attention to the details within our control to live a healthy and balanced lifestyle. During the last decade, through advances in medical science and prevention messaging, we all already know a number of things we could do to make ourselves healthier. The question of performance comes in when we look at our society and ask, "Why do some people work to live a healthy lifestyle, while others do not?" Performance in terms of a healthy lifestyle is not just for those who participate in athletic competition. It is clearly something all of us should desire. When you go to work, you will recognize and be informed of the risk factors that can get you into trouble in your job. How much more do we need to know the risk factors that will lead us toward disease and perhaps an unnecessarily early death?

Many individuals in our society, who overemphasize performance in external activities such as work, school, or sports, may not realize the importance of Performance-Driven Thinking in their personal life, which means their overall health and physical capability to perform will suffer. Ignoring the importance of performance in our personal lives within the area of health would be similar to going into an athletic event without the right equipment. Your personal performance is greatly tied to your ability to take care of yourself. Some of you reading this book need to revisit your personal health decisions, which will only lead to better performance in every area of your life. Smoking, overeating, and unhealthy addictions are just a few of the factors that interfere with Performance-Driven

Thinking. The way we take care of ourselves is clearly a matter of personal choice and performance.

## Personal Goals

The next area we will examine in the context of Performance-Driven Thinking is personal goal setting. What exactly do we mean by personal goals? When you were born, your parents had a number of personal goals for you. They began with your first steps, when everyone waited with baited breath for you to finally stop crawling and learn to walk. From there, the goal was learning to speak. Parents and grandparents alike could not wait for you to say your first words. From that point on, you were put on an automatic goal-setting pattern to journey up what could be called the educational mountain. This goal-setting pattern existed because in each grade you attended in school, you had to achieve certain standards in order to succeed. This continued until you completed the final step in your formal education—whether it was high school, college, graduate school, or any other level of higher education, and decided what you were going to do with your talents and abilities in the world.

This is when Performance-Driven Thinking becomes extremely important. Up to this point, your institution of learning and its leadership had set your performance goals for you. But after you achieve those educational performance goals, it's time to move toward the personal goals you must set for yourself. While trusted individuals and coaches, both in life and in work, can encourage and guide you in setting your personal goals, the responsibility is clearly your own.

So Performance-Driven Thinking becomes most relevant to our personal lives when we realize that goal setting is not just intended for education or work. Long-term successful performance can be clearly tied to an individual's ability to set personal performance goals within their own lives without an outside mandate. Many of us have had ideas about things that we can do within our own lives to increase our personal performance. But what tends to hold us back is the inability to set specific goals and initiatives that will help improve that personal performance. For example, many individuals after retirement age decide to go back to school for some kind of formal education. Clearly these individuals do not need this specific degree or certification as a work requirement. They decided to pursue a degree of higher learning to satisfy a personal, not a professional goal. This is clearly a result of Performance-Driven Thinking. These individuals, many of whom have retired and are on Social Security, wanted to achieve this particular goal for personal reasons, and they found the time, money, and energy to complete this goal.

Personal goals and Performance-Driven Thinking go hand in hand, due to the mere fact that once you become an adult, no one can force you to set personal goals. But what we do know is that in order to achieve peak personal performance, setting specific personal goals must be a vital part of who we are and how we operate. Some individuals don't set personal goals simply because they fear not meeting them. If you find yourself avoiding goal setting out of the fear of failure, then it's time to make failure your ally! See David's section on the "ugly ally" of failure in chapter 2. You can truly become a Performance-Driven Thinker by setting some form of personal goal outside of your work requirements. True Performance-Driven Thinkers embrace personal goal setting and enjoy the satisfaction of reaching beyond their current state and growing in their personal lives.

## Personal Relationships

Another critical area of Performance-Driven Thinking is personal relationships. Whether we want to admit it or not, our lives are deeply rooted in a number of personal relationships, such as family, marriage, or relationships with significant others. Unfortunately, based on the fact that over 50 percent of marriages within the United States alone end in divorce, one will not have to look far to discover the lack of Performance-Driven Thinking in this area. No one begins a specific relationship intending it to be unsuccessful. Even within the relationships we don't choose, such as family, most of us want positive relationships with our immediate and extended family members.

So, how does Performance-Driven Thinking impact our personal relationships? A great example would be the relationship between a parent and a child. Research clearly shows that the amount of time we spend with our children is closely linked to their success and adaptability as positive citizens in the future. But look at the number of parents who fail to spend quality time with their children. This issue has become increasingly difficult in this new "age of information." We know many teenagers experience little parental involvement. For the parents, this is clearly an issue of performance. Children do not arrive in our society by accident. Parenting requires performance. Performance-Driven Thinking is closely tied to our ability to parent successfully.

Here's another example. If you are currently in a marriage or significant relationship, I invite you to remember the first time you arranged to meet your partner. Did you dress sloppily? Did you fail to practice proper personal hygiene? Did you focus on yourself and your own needs, to the exclusion of your partner's? And then, as the relationship began to progress, did you begin insulting your partner and lack sensitivity? Of course not! When you found the person you wanted to spend a significant amount of soul-to-soul time with, you performed at a level that would make them want to engage you as a partner. The first impression you wanted to give this individual depended on your *performance*. You likely considered your dress, your manners, and the way you conducted yourself well before you rang the doorbell for the first time.

Most of us know that Performance-Driven Thinking is important when initiating personal relationships. But the real challenge is how we continue our performance as our personal relationships grow. One way we can address this issue is to continue to reinvest in what brought us together as partners in the first place. How did we perform in that first encounter? What could we do within our lives to replicate that style of thinking and performance? Doing so is quite possible if we simply choose to examine and measure our performance within our personal relationships. The failure of any personal relationship, whether family, marriage, or friendship, is closely tied not merely to our intentions but also to our performance. And the thinking that sustains these relationships is Performance-Driven Thinking.

## Personal Finance

The importance of Performance-Driven Thinking is perhaps most clear in the area of personal finance. If you have struggled to apply Performance-Driven Thinking to your personal finance, you may feel trapped in a form of financial prison. Your life may be held hostage by your financial decisions (or the lack thereof). In fact, if we lack Performance-Driven Thinking in our personal finances, it directly affects our performance in our personal relationships as well.

Our financial freedom is closely tied to our ability to practice Performance-Driven Thinking when managing our money and making financial decisions. Many people make financial decisions based on the means they wish they had rather than the means they actually have. Every professional investor you would talk to would clearly state that a person's financial independence is based solely on performance—not just that person's performance on the job, but their overall performance in making the right decisions to effectively manage and grow wealth in every context.

Every financial decision we personally make will be closely related to our ability to meet the financial requirements we have committed to make. This depends on performance. You cannot wish your way into financial performance; you have to think and plan your way into financial performance. In other words, you need Performance-Driven Thinking.

# Maintaining Balance When Setting Personal Goals

Although I wish to make the life of a Performance-Driven Thinker sound interesting, challenging, and rewarding to you, I wish to lead you not into temptation, but to deliver you from evil—especially as you begin setting your personal goals.

The temptation will be success. This may sound odd, especially since this whole book is about the importance of performance. Here's what I mean. When you incorporate Performance-Driven Thinking, success will be inevitable. When it comes, you're going to be nuts about it and you'll want more of it—the deluxe version. Go for it, but don't go with so much gusto that you destroy the balance in your life.

The evil will be your reactions to success. You may become solely motivated by the high profits that come with being an effective entrepreneur. You might change focus from the path of the Performance-Driven Thinker to the path of the work slave. Or worst of all, you might continue working without a plan.

Balance is the key to keeping temptations and evils at bay. It is the critical difference between a Performance-Driven Thinker and a traditional thinker. A Performance-Driven Thinker knows that unless balance is part of the overall plan right from the start, it's only going to be a word and never a style of living. Balance is very difficult to achieve if it's something you figure you'll get down the road. If you were on a high wire, balance is not something you'd settle for eventually. You'd want it always. You'd want it now. Life in today's environment is a high wire.

## Five Kinds of Work

**Performance-Driven Thinkers not only balance their work time with their leisure time, learning time, family time, and time for anything else they want to do, they also balance their work time itself, and they've learned that there are five kinds of work:**

**1. Wage work is job work.** In this scenario, you sell your time to the company employing you, and they manage your time. At one time, this work made the most sense for people. Your grandparents lived during that time, but it has passed. Wage work is nonsense for over half the people doing it now.

**2. Fee work is professional work.** Professionals in many fields charge a fee for the work they do and for their time, which is then spent the way they want, when they want, under their own management. People who work as consultants for businesses charge fees; they don't earn wages. This makes the business and the professional individuals satisfied.

**3. Housework is the work done on and for the home.** It's work that has to be done, such as cooking, cleaning, and shopping, and is ordinarily unpaid—and don't forget taking out the garbage! These days it is rapidly being redistributed from women to men. At the same time, it is more appreciated and is important enough to be part of a well-balanced work portfolio.

**4. Study work is educational work.** Self-improvement by way of an advanced degree or extra certification is more important than ever, as more people discover that a second or third degree gives them an edge in the working world. Performance-Driven Thinkers study to improve in many areas aside from work. Human understanding is part of what they learn.

**5. Volunteer work is free work.** You do this work for causes such as schools, hospitals, religious groups, political groups, charities, and sports groups. The income you derive from this work is emotional, spiritual, and permanent. To many people, it is more gratifying than financial income.

Performance-Driven Thinkers try to engage in all five kinds of work, knowing the benefits of each one will help them maintain balance. Wage work offers security; fee work provides the joy of being paid for your talent and knowledge; housework keeps you grounded; study work is an investment in yourself; volunteer work has the taxes paid by your body to your soul.

## A Built-in Balance Provider

How could you possibly fit all five kinds of work into your life? It's easy when *you plan at the outset*. Planning is a built-in balance provider. It helps ensure that you'll have time to help at home, to learn about life, and to help others while you bring home the bacon with your other pursuits—a regular gig a few days a week, or even once a month. If you do too much of any one kind of work, you'll be out of balance, and the work will almost instantly cease to be much fun. Today, Performance-Driven Thinkers achieve balance as a matter of choice, not as a matter of necessity.

Who leads the way in living unbalanced lives? Workaholics top the list. They often believe that unless they do their work immediately, the universe will come to a grinding halt. High achievers who sacrifice freedom come next on the list of unbalanced; they intentionally abandon balance for the sake of fame or fortune. Fame and fortune do have their price, but balance need not be part of it. Kids grow up only once. If you miss it the first time, there's no rerun.

Factory workers in the latter half of the twentieth century worked an average of forty hours per week. Unskilled laborers typically work only forty. But business owners average fifty-nine hours of work per week. What did these business owners have in mind when they opened their businesses? Certainly not a balanced structure for their work time and their free time. Certainly not an understanding of balance in life.

Some experts believe that workaholics are dying faster than alcoholics. This may not be readily apparent because so many workaholics watch their nutrition and exercise. They look great and may even work out regularly, but that only prolongs their ability to remain workaholics. They aren't listening to their bodies telling them something is wrong, so it takes something like a massive coronary to get their attention.

## World-Class Listeners

Performance-Driven Thinkers are exceptional listeners. They listen to their customers, to their mentors, to their friends, and to their kids. They listen to their parents and certainly to their teachers. They also listen to their bodies, their inner voice, the voice of reason. They never allow the past to dictate the future. In the past world of work, balance had no part, just as the idea of having enough time was not appreciated until the late 1980s. Although the idea of balance is finally on the forefront of the American mind, it is still a clouded notion, still a new concept, still considered an unattainable dream to many people. I believe that only two factors are required to achieve balance: to *imagine* it, and then to *commit* to it. Imagining it was harder than committing to it for me. Once I had visualized it, it was a relative cinch to commit to it.

The idea of visualizing balance is more "old age" than "new age." It is found in ancient texts. These writings state that success can be achieved effortlessly. Within every desire lie the mechanics of its fulfillment, its accomplishment. Wishing can breathe life into them. If I had read that before I had lived it, I would have thought that it was nonsense. Now I think it is common sense.

## Nature's Intelligence

As water automatically seeks its own level, intentions automatically seek their fulfillment if left alone. I'm not referring to the narrow intention of making a zillion bucks. Instead, I mean the broader intention that defines who you are—such as the intention to lead a balanced life.

Most people spend 99 percent of their time engaged in judgment and labeling other people according to their activities. If you stop doing that, you can begin to get in touch with your own potential—and that potential sure doesn't call for you to work for others forty hours a week or to work for yourself fifty-nine hours a week.

So don't be too narrow in your focus. The cost of wanting a result that is too specific is often stress and heart attacks. In America, by the time a person gets to the top, he's divorced, his kids are a mess, and his private life is in shambles. This is called success, but the person is miserable. Success should guarantee happiness as well. Doesn't that make sense to you? It makes sense to me, but does it make sense as to why financial success and emotional happiness so rarely co-exist?

To hit what you aim at, keep your attention on the present and orient yourself to the *process*, not to the *outcome*. If you focus on providing the finest product or the finest service, instead of concentrating solely on the bottom line, you will live according to your plan.

If your focus broadens to include doing what you love during your leisure time, family time, and other nonwork time, your plan will come vibrantly alive, and you will see clearly what you must do to keep it alive. I found it relatively simple to maintain this balance, through good times and bad. Once you step into paradise, it is not human nature to step out.

One of the most valuable requisites for creating balance is flexibility. Even as I tell you that I work only five days a week, I know good and well that I'll be flying to San Antonio this Thursday and speaking all day Friday. What about my balanced week? Out the window, that's what. *Almost* all my weeks are balanced weeks, but if I didn't have the flexibility to work five or seven days when the situation demanded my time, I'd be no Performance-Driven Thinker.

## The Smoky Room

Living and working a balanced life means knowing how to handle the periods of imbalance and uncertainty that characterize growth and beginning new ventures. Quentin Tarantino, the movie director, said upon completing his acclaimed film *Pulp Fiction*, "It was like entering a smoky room, then proceeding forward on faith even though I didn't see where I was going. Strictly faith kept me moving forward until the smoke began to vanish, and I could see everything clearly." He gave up perfect balance, experienced the uncertainty—but guided by his faith in himself and his intentions, he emerged with a sense of clarity and regained his balance.

Skiing is like that—it includes the sense of a controlled fall and feeling slightly out of balance almost all the time; yet you always catch yourself, restore your balance, and proceed at breakneck speed, propelled by gravity and faith in your ability. While you're skiing, there is certainly no time for drawn-out, rational thought. Often, regaining balance means moving fifty-eight sets of muscles in less than a quarter of a second. You can't think that through. Your body takes all its cues from your overall intention. Unless that *intention* is firmly planted in your heart and mind before you begin, you will find it very difficult to acquire it once you've established momentum. The idea is to maintain the momentum and to make balance part of the package.

You'll find it relatively easy to maintain balance if you begin with it. Start out with it *no matter what.* Don't delude yourself into thinking that you can switch gears later. Many have tried. Most have failed. Performance-Driven Thinkers are so enamored with the idea of balance that they wouldn't dream of losing sight of their target before they let the arrows fly. They know that once the arrows are in full flight, you can't say to them: "Okay, hang a left turn now!"

As a Performance-Driven Thinker, you're shooting an arrow. You get to take aim in any direction you want. If that direction does not include balance, you'll misfire. You will not be following the way of the Performance-Driven Thinker.

You realize by now that being a Performance-Driven Thinker is far more than pure work. It's really a work style, a lifestyle, a living style, a behavior style, a values style, a priorities style.

## Loving Your Leisure

If you don't have leisure activities that you love as much as your work, if you don't have a family or relationships that you enjoy every bit as much as your work, if you don't have the time to engage in leisure or bask in relationships, you're no Performance-Driven Thinker. For those are the elements that provide balance. You need them for equilibrium as much as you need the work itself.

I hope the above areas have given you a clear indication of how Performance-Driven Thinking can impact your personal life. Imagine a life where you completely neglected your personal health. Imagine a life where you were never driven to set personal goals. Imagine a life where you face total failure in all of your closest personal relationships. And imagine a life where you are totally over your head in debt and facing total financial crisis. All of these scenarios could come true if you don't include Performance-Driven Thinking in your personal life. You cannot improve your health, meet your personal goals, improve your personal relationships, or improve your financial capabilities without thinking about performance first. Personal Performance-Driven Thinking begins with the belief that *you control your own destiny* within your personal life. That destiny will be closely related to your ability to *think* about how you can be the best person you can be through your personal choices and lifestyle. So you see, you can't just perform at work if you want to have a totally fulfilled life. Performance-Driven Thinking begins at home.

**"What you get by achieving your goals is not as important as what you become by achieving your goals."**

**Zig Ziglar**

# Chapter 5:

Performance-Driven Thinking in Business

Today, in virtually every country around the world, people will flock to their jobs in an effort to increase the bottom-line profit of an organization. This goal of increased profits is the cornerstone of most, if not all, organized businesses. Yet the truth is that the average workers in most organizations have little awareness or concern about overall company profits. This leads to the following question: is a single financial measurement, such as quarterly profit, really the best indicator of a business's success?

I believe the answer is no. The success of a business starts way before the quarter ends. It begins every day with the arrival of each employee who will invest a certain amount of personal time and commitment in a particular business or organization. To measure a business's success, we must measure each employee's individual performance. Not only are we as individuals born to perform, but those of us who hold a job for an organization are also employed to perform. Imagine an organization that would employ individuals without expectation of performance on the job. No one wants to interview or reward a known non-performer. Clearly Performance-Driven Thinking belongs in the workplace.

At work, Performance-Driven Thinking begins with a sense of individual pride and our effort in producing measurable output. While some may think showing up at work and simply wasting time is a way to "get one over" on an organization or company, the truth is people who fail to perform actually cheat themselves. The knowledge, skills, and abilities you possess are yours for a reason and purpose. Moreover, when someone hires you, they are trusting you to exhibit your knowledge, skills, and abilities in the workplace. They are expecting a level of performance.

Needless to say, individual performance on the job becomes difficult in organizations that do not promote based on performance, or provide clear measurements for performance. Many organizations promote employees simply based on seniority or established relationships. Of course, the problem with this practice is that it encourages non-performance, no matter how you measure it.

Even though it may be difficult to become Performance Driven at work when few others seem to be measuring or pursuing high performance, it is possible. Here are the ten key steps to becoming a Performance-Driven Thinker at work:

1. Know your role.

2. Accept your role.

3. Play your role.

4. Identify workplace liabilities.

5. Build positive workplace relations.

6. Ask questions.

7. Seek opportunities.

8. Stay away from excuses.

9. Identify and learn from top performers.

10. Concentrate on performance and not systems.

The byproduct of this kind of Performance-Driven Thinking is a sense of loyalty to the overall mission and objectives of the organization. When we work hard to perform on behalf of a specific cause or goal, we begin to be a part of the overall mission. It is very difficult to be a top performer in an organization and not be connected to its overall focus and success. Individuals who are committed to the cause and mission of the company or organization not only tend to be top performers, but also tend to stay the course even during rough times. Company loyalty rarely happens for individuals who are not performance oriented. Individuals who simply go to work to go through the motions for the sole purpose of collecting a paycheck are typically not fully invested in the organization's mission. And the number of these individuals a company employs deeply impacts its bottom line.

# Measuring Success at Work as a Performance-Driven Thinker

Success at work as a Performance-Driven Thinker will be a lot more fulfilling than success at work in yesteryears. For example, if you're earning more money than you've ever imagined but are not content, you most assuredly are not experiencing success that comes from Performance-Driven Thinking. Success for the Performance-Driven Thinker will be measured by inner satisfaction more than any other criterion.

Perhaps that piece of soul can come from the work you do. It could also come from your leisure time and your achievements. Most likely it will be a combination, for a balanced life blends work with play. You won't be happy all of the time. If you were, you'd soon lose the edge necessary to succeed in a highly competitive century, one in which individuals (rather than huge corporations) will compete for time, attention, and dollars. Performance-Driven Thinkers always have that edge. But Performance-Driven Thinkers are happy more often than not.

Inner satisfaction is something you get not by seeking it, but by seeking work that ignites your passion and then doing that work. It is a realization that occurs rather than a consciously sought attainment. But you won't realize it by chasing money or even by getting money, no matter how much you make.

Along with inner satisfaction, the Performance-Driven Thinker will orient his business towards being with his family—the small nuclear family of yesterday, as well as the larger extended family of today. He will become part of his community, whether that community is his neighborhood, his industry, or his online world. He will obtain much of the fun he needs from the work he does, but he will also recognize he needs recreation beyond work. Surely he will be motivated by the old goals of financial independence, control of his destiny, and recognition of his talents. But he will also be drawn to a newer goal best described as innovation or discovery. He will want to contribute to society with more than his time or money. Through the work he does, he will find ways to do this, because Performance-Driven Thinkers are resourceful. In fact, resourcefulness is a survival technique of the Performance-Driven Thinker.

## A Performance-Driven Roadmap

The Performance-Driven Thinker is able to succeed on the journey by having a clear and simple roadmap. Performance-Driven signposts illuminate the road. Here's what they say.

- Learn

- Cooperate

- Focus

- Feel passion

- Delegate

- Share

- Respect time

- Bend

- Profit

- See

These signposts enable Performance-Driven Thinkers to select their pace and never lose their way. Performance-Driven Thinkers realize that even after they have passed a sign, they continue to move in the right direction. They keep in mind the words on these additional signposts:

- Plan

- Manage

- Market

- Sell

- Serve

- Satisfy

- Relate

- Globalize

- Improve

- Be cool

## What Promotes Happiness

Since Performance-Driven Thinkers strive to achieve inner satisfaction, the components of happiness are well known to them. In his book *The Pursuit of Happiness*, author David Myers, sounding a lot like a Performance-Driven Thinker, cites ten items that promote happiness.

1. A fit and healthy body

2. Realistic goals and expectations

3. Positive self-esteem

4. Feelings of control

5. Optimism

6. Outgoingness

7. Supportive friendships

8. An intimate, sexually warm marriage of equals

9. Challenging work and active leisure coupled with adequate rest and retreat

10. Spiritual faith

We are living in a time when people are just beginning to turn down promotions, to quit the corporate rat race to start businesses for themselves, to move to less stressful environments, to pursue less demanding careers. People are taking a new look at the meaning of success. They no longer automatically assume that the only way to be successful is to always be moving up the corporate ladder, to be burning the midnight oil.

An employee survey by Levi Strauss showed that 79 percent wanted more flexibility to set their own work schedules. "Presumably," says a personnel director, "so they can spend more time with their families and pursue other interests."

## A Spawning Ground for Performance-Driven Thinkers

Just yesterday, America's economy was based on companies that made more and more of the same product at lower and lower prices. Today the economy is based on companies that quickly provide customized products and services to meet the tailored needs of small, neat groups of consumers.

Fortunately, such an economy is a natural spawning ground for Performance-Driven entrepreneurs.

**Learn to love your network.** In the past, Americans would measure success by their ability to climb the corporate ladder. But that ladder exists no more. Success is measured by the results of your creativity, your autonomy, and your ability to devise a new solution, develop a new idea, deliver a new service. Often success is achieved by teams. At the conclusion of a project, the teams disband and the people move on to other teams. The ladder is now a network—an infinite number of paths that ultimately connect with many others. Rather than trudge from one wrong path to the next on a rigid upward course, you can connect with others at lightning speed and then disconnect when your purposes have been achieved. The larger your network, the more work will come your way. The better you treat other members of the network, the better they'll treat you. As in the past, people who are fun to work with will be at a premium. Prima donnas and mean-spirited, high-achievers need not apply in the world of the Performance-Driven Thinker.

**What you earn depends more than ever upon what you learn.** You can do your learning at a college, technical school, or training on the job. In California, enrollment in community colleges has soared by 300 percent in the past three decades. A woman with a community college degree earns 33 percent more than her counterpart with only a high school diploma. For men the figure is 26 percent more money. Security no longer comes from sticking with one company for an entire career, but by maintaining a portfolio of flexible skills. That's why there are so many universities out there offering lifelong learning classes to students from college age through golden age, online and offline. The new economy will not be a dog-eat-dog economy, but a skill-eat-skill economy. The more skills you have and the better trained you are with the skills you have, the more success you will achieve—pure cause and effect.

*In Search of Excellence* author Tom Peters calls Performance-Driven Thinkers to action. He says, "The only way to lose is to not try. Not every big firm is a Walmart or a CNN. Not every firm will be around in the future. But the trend is unmistakable. Frankly, I don't know how to do much more than exhort, 'Build your own firm, and create your own network'—it's that or bust."

## Care Like Crazy

Says Peters of the future, "Add it up and you get something rather surprising. There's no rejection of the past in all this! Expertise is more important than ever, not less. And bigness has its place. However, expertise is being changed, altered almost beyond recognition. If you're not skilled/motivated/passionate about something, you're in trouble!" Notice this—the man did not say what you're to be skilled, or motivated, or passionate about—that's for you to determine. He only advises that you *care like crazy about it.*

So the magic question is, as a leader or member of a company or organization, how do you drive individuals to work-related Performance-Driven Thinking? A bigger question is, how do you develop a workplace culture of Performance-Driven Thinkers?

The first step in achieving this goal is to create a hiring process that would reliably select the most qualified and energetic candidates suited to the mission of the organization. This includes selecting the individuals who clearly indicate they are self-motivated, self-starters, and self-achievers, and they thrive on celebrating accomplishments. As a result, you will notice an energy in your organization that will soon translate into visible performance.

The second step is adequate training. Yes, we believe that organizations should train all their employees in Performance-Driven Thinking. We can no longer expect employees to naturally perform their job functions at top levels without the proper training and leadership.

The third step is to develop Performance-Driven leadership. In the next chapter we will discuss the specifics of how to lead an organization of Performance-Driven Thinkers.

So the process of creating a Performance-Driven workplace comes down to the following basics: we employ motivated and qualified individuals, train them to be Performance-Driven Thinkers, and then encourage them by training the organization's leadership on how to drive and lead performance. The combined magic of Performance-Driven Thinkers at the line level and Performance-Driven coaches at the leadership level will equal a Performance-Driven workplace culture.

"I couldn't find the sports car of my dreams so I built one."

Ferdinand Porsche

# CHAPTER 6:

## *Leading Performance-Driven Thinking*

Performance-Driven Thinking in the workplace requires developing and exhibiting the right skills in leadership. Historically, leadership in most organizations has meant closely evaluating the actions and work performance of individuals serving as line performers in the group under the leader's management. Yet leaders need to practice Performance-Driven Thinking, too. As we move into decision-making positions in our organization, performance means not just attaining a position but serving as a leader. Leading Performance-Driven Thinking in the workplace may help you develop the necessary skillset it takes to move your organization from good to great.

Some years ago, management focused on evaluating workplace ethics and production of the people doing the everyday work, with little regard for the overall day-to-day performance of the managers themselves. During this time period, many organizations began training and developing managers without closely examining what it takes to lead by performance. Yet no one wants to work for an individual they do not feel is not competent to provide more than mere management. People in the workplace and in our society today crave not managers, but real leaders—which means they need to believe their leaders deserve to be in the position they're in. Performance-Driven Thinking is in fact one ingredient that distinguishes managers from leaders. Performance-Driven Thinking in leadership begins when individuals called to pave the way for the organization are truly Performance Driven, and in observing their actions, the workers realize that the true measurement of their skills is also based on how they perform.

Again, let's examine how organizations are typically run in our society. In most organizations, policies and procedures systems are in place for people who come to work every day. Part of these systems includes the use of employee evaluation procedures. With this age-old process, individuals in key positions within an organization have been able to separate employees who possess a higher degree of work ethic from those who simply pursue the status quo. However, for many of those who exhibited an apparently lower work ethic than their peers, the key issue may not have been inability to achieve the desired standards of the organization, but a lack of leadership.

In too many organizations we are quick to promote and maintain individuals in key positions without regard to proven performance. This dilemma has created a world of too many managers and not enough leaders—and employees' performance suffers. Leading Performance-Driven Thinking takes more than just reading this book or attending what has been termed "management seminars."

It requires action, and that action could set you apart within your organization as a true leader and not just another manager.

# Measuring Success as a Performance-Driven Leader

A Performance-Driven Leader is one who not only helps others be successful, but also models success. Yet so many people have never taken the time to define what success is for them, whether it's at work, in their relationships, in their volunteer activities, or in their personal pursuits. Here is how Performance-Driven Leaders measure success in business, both for themselves and for those they lead:

As in anything else, the first factor in measuring success in business is to assess your inner satisfaction, to determine whether you are enjoying the process of working or even enjoying being alive. The second factor is to ascertain whether your work meshes well with your life, as well as your essence, or who you really are. The third factor is to determine whether or not you have balance in your life.

And there's a fourth measurement of your success—*after* you've arranged to have enough free time, *after* you've found ways to contribute to your planet, *after* you've formed your connections, *after* your relationships are in order and your health is excellent. This measuring method should be part of your overall plan, or you'll lose your way.

The yardstick to which I refer is *profits*, the lifeblood of a business. Performance-Driven Leaders keep their eyes on that bottom line, but they never lose their awareness of their higher priorities.

Amazingly, some businesses *never* address this crucial yardstick. Even more ridiculous, many businesses make this the *only* criterion of their success. The way of the Performance-Driven Leader gives this measure of success a modified priority. Performance-Driven Leaders are inevitably interested in this measurement because it is an important part of why they are in business in the first place. But they never give profits the highest priority, because profits are neither the only nor the most important reason for being in business.

## More Important than Profits

Here are ten things that true Performance-Driven Leaders consider to be more important than profits:

1. Their future

2. Their overall plan

3. Their customers

4. Their employees

5. Their prospects

6. Their families

7. Their time

8. Their inner satisfaction

9. Their integration of business and life

10. Their balance

## Less Important than Profits

Now, here are ten things that true Performance-Driven Thinkers consider less important than profits:

1. Their sales

2. Their turnover

3. Their response rate

4. Their store traffic

5. Their volume

6. Their gross

7. Their press coverage

8. Their ego

9. Their status quo

10. Their growth

The thousands of workers laid off each year in this country represent *families* who have lost their security—families displaced by companies finally facing up to the reality of profits. If more companies went the way of the Performance-Driven Leaders, and put more of a premium on the almighty profit, more families would be spared the pain of layoffs.

For what are profits? They are what is left over after the business expenses have been paid. In reality, they are whatever the business owner *determines* them to be. Is that leased Porsche the owner's personal financial responsibility, allowing the profits to remain high—or is it a business expense that is deducted from the profits? The owner's answer determines her profit margin.

## Performance-Driven Leaders Don't Kid Themselves

Performance-Driven Leaders never kid themselves. They know that big isn't necessarily better, that expensive isn't necessarily worth the extra expense. They perform two primary jobs that increase their profits:

- They improve everything they do.

- They eliminate any mistakes entirely.

Performance-Driven Leaders have a wide definition of *everything*—it consists of anything connected with their business, inside and out. They have an equally broad definition of *mistakes*. Anything that is not done with excellence is a mistake. Performance-Driven Leaders are not perfectionists, knowing that perfectionists cause stress for others and can be ineffective in their use of time. Performance-Driven Leaders do have high standards and noble expectations. They expect those standards to be met without exception. They take for granted that their expectations will be met, and often exceeded.

The Performance-Driven Leader knows that improvements increase profits, and mistakes decrease profits.

What do the corporate instigators of the downsizing era have to say about their reprehensible but unavoidable behavior? "It was one of the hardest things I've ever done. I felt like I was personally contributing to the recession," says the CEO of a large software company. If he had it to do over, he "would have hired at a more conservative rate. I would have planned fewer projects. I would have focused and done a few things well."

Right now (a clear indication that the time is right for entrepreneurs to become guerrillas, flourish, and succeed), almost half of all US workers are employed in industries that are shedding jobs. The public sector is also cutting back. For every person put out of work because of the cyclical nature of the economy—being fired, quitting, or retiring—*three* are cut as corporations restructure. Those corporations have made their mistakes before. They are not going to make them again.

Most companies want Performance-Driven Leaders but are not sure how to develop them. In years past, organizations practiced a top-down, dictator-style of leadership. This style made it easier for those in charge to simply hide behind their titles. This whole style was based on a "just do as I say" theory that in many cases alienated the baseline workforce. People were led to believe that interaction with leadership was a certain way to bring doom and gloom to one's career. This so-called "us against them" attitude was a clear indictment against performance and leadership. In addition, it impacted workplace loyalty and morale.

With the rise of a new, more creative workforce, the expectations of organizational leadership has clearly shifted to performance. Leaders are driven to perform. Managers are driven to maintain. So leaders are not threatened by creativity the way managers might be. The "barking orders" mentality of top-down management is quickly being replaced with a performance-based model. This new leadership style is based on valuing a "let's work together" type of atmosphere. To put it simply, management is shifting to real leadership, and the "just do what I say" style is shifting to a leadership style that values performance for leaders as well as employees.

One might ask, "Is this style of leadership possible in a company or organization?" The answer is clearly yes, if the following formula is put into place:

1.  Train all personnel in Performance-Driven Thinking. This will allow for a culture shift in the organization, which in turn will help develop leaders.

2. Train all managers and leaders in Performance-Driven Leadership. This will allow all managers and leaders to operate from the same perspective and values.

3. Change leadership evaluations to make them more performance and production based.

4. Allow for constant employee feedback. This will ensure performance continuity across the various organizational levels.

We truly believe that with the influx of Performance-Driven Thinking in the workplace and the training of Performance-Driven Leaders, all organizations can develop a culture of Performance-Driven production.

**"You can't build a reputation with what you are going to do."**

**Henry Ford**

# Chapter 7:

## Dealing with Non-Performers

Many of you may already agree with the Performance-Driven Thinking perspective. Perhaps even some of you feel very strongly that, whether in personal or work-related issues, you already give more than 100 percent. To you, we say, "Bravo!" But perhaps you're also wondering, "What about those slackers who work with me, and just will not perform?" What are we supposed to do with others who just don't seem to get it?

This is a very challenging yet important area to deal with. We've already mentioned that the lack of performance is extremely contagious. It can quickly become a roadblock to those who have the initiative to be top performers. We could say, "Just don't pay attention to non-performers, and just focus on your own performance." But we know it's not that easy.

As I mentioned in chapter 1, I spent many years working as a member of my hometown police department. As part of the local government, no matter how hard anyone within our organization worked, in the end all of us were going to get the same 1, 2, or 3 percent increase as everyone else. To add further insult to the idea of performance, each employee was evaluated one time a year without any additional job feedback. This system, which is still in practice today, simply allows non-performers to prosper.

When people are rewarded for presence only and not performance, it creates an easy road that can have a negative impact on Performance-Driven Thinking. As a matter of fact, while working in the police department, I found that many times those who showed initiative and creativity were looked at as problem individuals within the system. We discussed this line of thinking in chapter 2, in the context of America's love affair with entitlement. So the fact is that even some of our job-related evaluation processes could be encouraging non-performance. For individuals who choose to live out the philosophy of Performance-Driven Thinking, pursuing performance within this climate can become extremely frustrating.

Performance-Driven individuals thrive not only on having clear expectations, but knowing when they have exceeded those expectations. Dealing with non-performers requires not only setting clear expectations, but also ensuring others are aware of when they are not meeting those expectations. The first rule is broken when individuals do not clearly know or understand their expectations. The second rule is ignored when leadership fails to confront non-performers for their lack of meeting what is expected. In situations where this is occurring, the need for a leadership climate change becomes necessary. Simply stated, in any setting in life, treating performers like non-performers establishes a morale issue that can quickly impact the quality of any environment.

There is not a business leader in America who would not agree with the following statement: "I want to increase employee performance and bottom-line production." At the same time, these same leaders fail to set required expectations and hold people accountable to performance. This problem, if not dealt with, can significantly impact organizational retention and succession. To put it in plain terms, top performers will not stay where they feel their ability to grow is blocked by a failed system that embraces non-performance.

An example of this in action would simply require a visit back into the world of sports. Think of how many top-performing athletes have left one franchise to join another simply for a chance to win a championship. Many of these players could simply have stayed at top dollar within the cities they were playing. But for the sake of joining a winning situation, players have decided to leave what they know for what they want to achieve. While we may find fault with this thinking, it is clearly an example of Performance-Driven Thinking.

Non-performers in life and in business are intimidated by top performers. But they also fail to recognize that being around individuals at the top of their game can only make us better. Throughout my many years as a coach, I have encouraged people within their personal, business, and athletic lives to take on greater challenges. Remaining at a weak level of performance simply does not allow us to grow. Just like an athletic team that plays a weak schedule, individuals who thrive on dominating weakness in the name of performance do not reach their goals.

A great example is, again, from the world of sports. Teams are chosen every year during the month of March to participate in the NCAA basketball playoffs. Two of the key factors in selecting a team are its strength and scheduling. Just as in life, those who choose to play in a weaker field do not gain the rewards of those who choose to face challenges.

While non-performers are not interested in selecting avenues that will give them the greatest challenges, performers can't wait to embrace them. So another key way to deal with non-performers in life is to showcase the clear rewards that come from facing greater challenges. Just like non-performance is contagious, so is Performance-Driven Thinking. How do you make people better? How do you increase the output of non-performers? How do you take people to a place where they can achieve beyond belief? You surround them with performers. You build your organization on performance through your values, work ethic, and core leadership. Simply changing the climate of what's expected and the accountability regarding those expectations, along with an increased focus and a true commitment to values, work ethic, and core leadership, will help bring even the non-performers into the eventual light of performance.

# Others Not Performing?
# Improve Your Delegation Skills!

If Performance-Driven Leaders discover that the performance of those they're working with doesn't meet the high standards they expect, they don't get frustrated or try to micromanage. Neither do they relax their standards. **Performance-Driven Leaders view this situation as an opportunity to improve their delegating skills.**

*Delegating* is a word that everybody knows, but few people practice delegation with skill. Performance-Driven Thinkers are masters at passing the buck, empowering others, and achieving high-level results. To be as adept as they are, to put your delegating money where your delegating mouth is, consider the following ideas:

Recognize that every time you delegate successfully, you are doubling your own effectiveness.

Unless a task is your passion, don't do it if you can delegate it. Recognize that you are delegating not only work, but also responsibility for results.

Don't delegate a task to someone who won't do the work as well or better than you could do it.

Don't delegate a task to someone if you're not willing to first train that person to do the job with excellence.

Don't always tell the person to whom you are delegating *how* to achieve the results. Just talk about the results to encourage initiative.

Don't limit the concept of delegating work only to work chores; consider it also for the multitude of home chores. Time is time—always precious.

When delegating, provide as much information about the task as possible, but don't overload a person with data.

When you delegate, be sure that you also delegate the authority to make the necessary related decisions. Let the person to whom you delegate set the terms, timetables, and objectives so he or she can measure how the work is going.

Tell the truth about a task to the person to whom you delegate it. If it is drudgery, don't say that the task is glamorous.

If you don't know how to trust, you'll have problems delegating. True Performance-Driven Thinkers have the ability to trust others with territory and power.

When you elevate your delegating skills to the level that work delegated is work accomplished *better* than you would have done it, you'll be able to structure your business to be compatible with your nature. This invaluable talent will set you apart from entrepreneurs of the past.

So if you notice the performance of others around you is not up to par, perhaps they don't have enough information, or authority, or trust from you. Perhaps you've misrepresented the nature of a task to encourage them to accept the responsibility. If you can diagnose your delegation problems and fix them, the performance of others around you will surely increase.

Let's face it. Even though we have been led to believe that people will automatically perform to their highest ability within a system that does not actively promote performance, we now know that this is far from the truth. So if our system across the board has not been effective in encouraging performance, then we really can't find tremendous fault with non-performers individually. People tend to operate at a level they are allowed to remain in. Simply speaking, when it comes to non-performers, workplace climate and culture cannot be separated. If within your organization non-performers make up a significant part of your culture, what room do performers exist in?

I teach the simple philosophy that culture sets climate. What you allow to exist within your organization—including non-performance—simply becomes the climate of your organization. Nothing expected equals nothing given. Despite the common false belief that non-performing individuals in the age of entitlement are happy people, an organization must create a different culture based on a true belief, and start to embrace Performance-Driven Thinking once and for all.

"There are people that have more talent than you do, but there is no excuse for anyone to work harder than you do."

**Derek Jeter**

# CHAPTER 8:

## Believing in Small Wins

As many people set out to establish the goal of performing better, one common frustration is the feeling of lack of accomplishment. This feeling could come from a culture that makes us think any achievement short of a major, newsworthy accomplishment doesn't qualify as performance. However, it is critical to sustain a positive attitude toward performance, because winning does not happen overnight, and championships are normally not won in a week. So the question remains: how can you maintain the drive within your personal and professional life that will allow you to stay on the path of sustaining performance? The concept that will allow you to continue your drive is the Small Wins theory.

The Small Wins theory stresses the point that very few achieve overnight success, regardless of what their specific personal or specific goal may be. In our education system, the idea that a failing student could become a student of excellence within a month's time is unrealistic. In reality, the failing student, with the right drive and determination, could actually become a passing student within that same period of time. Even though the student may not achieve the highest goal of excellence, the focus on *progress* in performance is leading this individual in the right direction.

Consider the individual who suddenly develops the desire to lose weight. The overall goal of this individual is to lose up to thirty pounds within a specific period of time. After a short time passes, the individual realizes that they have lost a total of almost ten pounds. Would we not consider this "small win" to be a performance worth noting, as a significant step toward the overall goal? The runner training for a half-marathon who improves their time on a 5K run should be viewed as performing in the right direction. The examples of people all around us improving their skills, even when they have not yet reached their overall personal and professional goals, are endless.

So sometimes the problem isn't a lack of accomplishment. The problem may be a culture that does not recognize performance outside of total victory. This "all or nothing" thinking undermines the concept of Performance-Driven Thinking. Individual and professional goals were not set for overnight success. Goal setting takes a sustained attitude of performance. The idea of "one and done" performance, in most instances, is unlikely and unsustainable, and many times leads to mental and emotional defeat. It becomes too easy to give up Performance-Driven Thinking when we do not instantly receive the big trophy. The idea of small wins in reality means that any growth in our personal or professional performance is really a victory. We can sustain our Performance-Driven Thinking when we embrace those small victories and count them as wins.

# Money in This New Millennium

Not making enough money fast enough can be discouraging for the entrepreneur. As we consider the importance of small wins in sustaining performance, we also need to consider that the Performance-Driven Thinker has a different view of money than most.

Money is not the root of all evil. What George Bernard Shaw really said is that *lack of money* is the root of all evil, and what the Bible actually says is that the *love of money* is the root of all evil. Money itself is completely innocent of all charges.

I have stated and reiterated that information is the currency, the money of this new century. That is the truth. And it is your first indication that money will come in many forms as we evolve. The biggest change between the twentieth century and the twenty-first century comes not in money, but in the way we perceive money, and how much we allow it to dictate our lives. Although important, money will not be the top item on our mission statement if we're a Performance-Driven Thinker. Enough money will be one goal, but more than enough money can get you in trouble.

Philosopher and psychologist Gregory Bateson said that "Humans must have balanced relationships with everything on earth. If we don't have enough magnesium in our systems, we will be in big trouble. If we have too much, it will be toxic to us. If we have the right amount, all will be well." The same thing is true for money. Not enough is a problem. Too much can be toxic. The right amount to cover a person's needs is comfortable and healthy. Performance-Driven Thinkers are not blinded by money and know when enough is enough. I'm not saying that they are Spartan. No way. But I do want to plant the notion that money should be seen in its proper perspective. It is not the key to life. It is not the key to the universe.

This is not to say that enlightened businesses no longer list money as a major priority. Instead, cash is no longer the number-one priority. It is not disdained, only reduced in rank. And it has changed in form as well. Not all of it can be folded.

Increasing numbers of workers in America are opting to take their money in the form of free time, healthier surroundings, or better working conditions. They are settling for lower salaries in exchange for working fewer hours. They are choosing to be paid less money in return for living in a community with clean air, a more natural outdoor environment and lower prices. They are selecting opportunity over income. Money is no longer the entire target, but part of the target.

Some money transactions will take the form of barter. Barter is one of the fastest-growing segments of the US economy. In 2005, 55 percent of all the media purchased in America isn't really purchased; it was bartered for. For a great snapshot of the art of barter, check out Ali Pervez and Dave Wagenvoord's book *No Cash? No Problem!* to learn how to get everything you want in business and life, without using cash.

In a world where everyone measures wealth with money and success with obtaining the top position, anything less in many instances is not noticed or applauded. We are too busy celebrating the big championships to notice that success is really happening in the everyday wins of progressive, positive performance. As we mentioned above, our biggest opponent to the small wins theory is the current dominant culture. This opponent has caused many people to give up their goals and life's dreams. But we also participate in our own failure whenever we measure our success against that of other people and their current position or aspirations.

In order for us to truly embrace Performance-Driven Thinking, we can't simply blame the culture. We must ensure that we attack our opponent on an individual basis. The minute we start comparing ourselves and our circumstances to others, we instantly create an even bigger opponent to performance and success. The theory of small wins is based on not how your neighbors or coworkers perform and succeed, but on how you perform and succeed. It is easy to feel as if you are not performing if you only focus on where you are now and your current circumstances. Performance-Driven Thinking is about not just focusing on where you currently are, but where you have the possibility to be. In addition, Performance-Driven Thinking is not about the end result, but next result. Are you performing better today than you did yesterday? And will you be performing better tomorrow than you did today? In order to sustain our performance, many times we have to switch our focus from the big picture or goal to the next picture or goal.

Earlier I mentioned the struggling boys' middle school basketball team I had the opportunity to coach in my local community. As a coach, I would have loved to have walked into the gym for the first time, with a team that had not won a game in several seasons, and assure them that we would win the championship. But for me to get these young men to focus on performance, I had to build our goal on a foundation of reality. To tell this team we were going to win the championship would have been to inspire false hope. Instead, I set as our first goal the simple belief that our team could win at least one game. Following our first victory, the players began to believe in the concept of performance and winning more games. This thinking among these young men became contagious, and as I reported earlier, we went on to win a total of nine games that season. So the key to this and all success regarding performance is to realize the possibilities while balancing the possibilities with reality.

The Small Wins theory is completely compatible with Performance-Driven Thinking. The Small Wins theory does not mean that you lose sight of the big picture. It means that, while keeping the big picture in mind, you understand that it is all right to feel very positive about the series of steps that will get you to the big picture. Do not wait to celebrate performance at the end of the road to your goal or dream. Make a habit of celebrating the small wins every day of your life. This is truly Performance-Driven Thinking.

**"You can't win a championship without winning the next game."**

**Bobby Kipper**

# CHAPTER 9:

## Sustaining Performance-Driven Thinking

Now that we've discussed the Small Wins theory, it's a good time to discuss other issues that can impact how well we can sustain our performance over time. Most of us would agree that performance tends to come and go, whether in our personal or professional lives. We've all experienced those days when we wake up with a renewed sense of energy and urgency to accomplish our goals and dreams. At the end of those kinds of days, we typically recognize we have accomplished a great deal, and we have a good feeling about our overall progress. Perhaps you can recall some of these specific days when you were on top of the world due to your accomplishments.

While this feeling is good and is essential to a successful life, we all must agree that the opposite feeling has occurred in each of us at some point. We can all recall days when we felt very slow to perform, and we lacked the energy and the initiative to get it done. During these days, we realize that we have wasted time and not produced the necessary performance to move on to the next level. Therefore, the next magic question in our journey to performance is, "What distinguishes a day of accomplishments from a day of wasted opportunity?" In other words, what separates people in our society who are "sitting on G and waiting on O," ready and eager to move forward, from those lacking the ability to perform?

We have learned that Performance-Driven Thinking is the mental awareness that embraces the effort to get results. So in order to employ this style of thinking on a regular basis, we must work at sustaining this thinking in both our personal and professional lives. It is too easy to use the scapegoat excuse of "I am having another bad day." The way to sustain Performance-Driven Thinking is to intentionally make it part of your mental, emotional, and action thought process on a daily basis.

Sustaining performance is no easy task, especially when you take it out of the context of sports and the performing arts. But perhaps we should follow their lead even in our daily performance at work, home, or in the community. After all, athletic teams train daily to get ready for the performance on the field or court that is to come. Musical performers rehearse consistently before they put on the big show. To help you to focus on sustaining Performance-Driven Thinking, we have come up with ten basic steps to assist you in the process. These ten steps, while not foolproof, will certainly go a long way to ensuring that you spend many more days performing than remaining idle.

## 1. Set Reachable Personal and Professional Goals

Earlier in the process of describing Performance-Driven Thinking, we talked about the importance of setting personal and professional goals. In addition, we introduced you to the concept of meeting basic goals and also reaching stretch goals. Sustaining performance will depend on ensuring that each goal you set is certainly within your ability to achieve. While we agree that lofty goal setting is both challenging and exciting, it can also be defeating. If, during the process of trying to reach your goal, you realize that it is beyond your capability, this will have a major impact on your morale and therefore your ability to perform long term. Simply revise your goal to something more realistic, and go for it!

## 2. Develop Milestones in the Process

As an example of the Small Wins theory we introduced earlier, one way to sustain your Performance-Driven efforts is to identify specific milestones along the way toward reaching your overall goal. Simply having the major goal in your sights without identifying the intermediate steps toward the goal is like trying to find a location for the first time without directions. Milestones in our journey to sustained performance function like a roadmap that directs our course of travel.

## 3. Identify When You Reach Each Milestone

It is not enough to have stated steps along the way toward your overall goal of performance. If you don't recognize when you are making progress toward the overall goal, you will significantly hamper your chances of achieving your goal. To put it simply, to set specific milestones without realizing you have achieved them is like a runner trying to complete a race while only running in place. Take, for example, distance runners who participate in various road races such as 5Ks, half-marathons, and marathons. Anyone who is familiar with this process knows all along the race route there are indicators of how far you have traveled. For many runners, this is not only an indication of how much further they have to go, but a motivation to keep going. The same mindset can be used as we deal with performance in our everyday lives. No matter what our goal or specific action is, it will be easier to continue pursuing when we recognize we are continually reaching the milestones we set toward that goal.

## 4. Chart Your Actions to Reach the Next Step

Once you realize that you have reached a specific milestone, you must create a mental process to evaluate and chart out steps to the next milestone. Many times, while performing, we tend to lose our way because we have not charted out a plan of action. Setting a specific course toward each objective along the way will help us to sustain our performance mindset.

## 5. Identify Multiple Paths to Reach Your Next Milestone

One of our greatest opponents in sustaining Performance-Driven Thinking is when we have planned a course of action to the next milestone that ends up unsuccessful. This is when sustaining our mental commitment to performance gets harder to maintain. Just as there are several routes to most destinations, there are several paths to reach most milestones en route to your overall goal. Life is full of mental, emotional, and physical setbacks. When we chart multiple paths to success, many times our difficulties become temporary and minimal. In the words of one wise man, when you come up against a life-altering opponent, to be successful you may have to focus on building a bridge and getting over it. When life's road to performance is blocked, think ahead to identify multiple paths to success to sustain your Performance-Driven Thinking.

## 6. Surround Yourself with Positive Influences to Encourage You

Many people go through life with the desire to perform, but at the same time they continually put themselves in an underdog position even before they start. Many things can prevent us from claiming life's Performance-Driven victory, but one of the greatest is our inability to see the negative influences within our own lives. Truly no one can sustain a positive attitude toward performance if they surround themselves with people who do not believe in them or their goals, or have the ability to be positive about life in general. This isn't just about connecting to people who believe the glass is "half full." People who believe a glass is half full have a 50 percent chance of losing every day. Why would we want to be around people whose attitudes and beliefs mean they only have a 50 percent chance of succeeding?

In sports, if you want to develop into a better player, you surround yourself with players with a greater talent level than you have developed. To sustain Performance-Driven Thinking, the same is true. Several years ago, I personally went through a life-changing experience, dealing with divorce and the breakup of my family. What rescued me, and helped pave my road back to performance, was my ability to surround myself with positive people. Take the example of a car battery. The spark to ignite new energy does not come from the negative grounding side of the battery, but it comes from the positive side of the battery. The same thing is true about the drive to perform. The road becomes a great deal smoother when we are daily plugged into positive people-related energy, which enhances our performance. In addition, this will go a long way in helping us sustain our Performance-Driven Thinking.

## 7. Work through Your Opposition

Earlier in the book, we talked about identifying your opponents. Once you have identified what opposes you and have designed multiple ways to approach your opposition, your ability to sustain Performance-Driven Thinking comes down to your will to succeed. In reality, you already have decided what you want. When life opposes you, you have to decide how badly you want it. Facing the reality that you will encounter daily opposition in your journey toward performance, and preplanning accordingly, will help you to sustain your Performance-Driven Thinking.

## 8. Focus on Good Time Management

Another obstacle on our road to performance is the age-old problem of effective time management. There are only twenty-four hours in each day, and a certain number of those hours are required for proper rest. Therefore, it is important to understand that performance, if done in the right way, demands time management. No one ever reaches their goals by procrastination and failing to use proper time management skills. On the road to performance, it is very easy to get sidetracked by issues and problems that take us away from the journey to our goal. No one ever improved their personal or professional skills by waiting until tomorrow. The time to perform is now, and in order to reach your personal or professional goals, that time has to be planned and treated as sacred. (See David's sidebar below for more on time management.)

## 9. Evaluate Your Process

So now that you understand how to properly set goals, plan your journey toward performance, and feel encouraged and motivated to get started, how will you know if you are going in the right direction? Just as it's important to plan out the journey toward your goals, it is equally as important to evaluate your path along the journey. The key to any successful performance lies in constantly evaluating your growth toward your overall goal. Many people fear the thought of evaluation because we tend to make that aspect of goal setting much too difficult. Evaluating your performance can begin with simply assessing your overall feeling about how you are progressing in the process. By selecting the self-measurement criteria that are simple yet meaningful to us, we can all get to a position where we know that progress is occurring. At the same time, the evaluation process will quickly let us know if we need to change directions.

## 10. Set Your Next Goal

So now you have applied all the information we have shared with you about performance, and you find that in your personal and professional life you begin to reach new heights and have met the goals you have set for yourself through solid Performance-Driven Thinking. You realize it is time to set additional goals for yourself. Living life without something to strive for creates an empty shell of the performance for an individual. To truly sustain performance, you must continually be striving toward a specific goal or accomplishment.

# Structuring Your Time: The Key to Sustainable Performance

If you're already a Performance-Driven Thinker, you don't need to be reminded that time is not money. If time ever was money, it certainly isn't anymore. Time is far more important than money. If you run out of money, there are countless ways to scrounge up more. If you run out of time, it's RIP.

The key to sustaining performance in business and in life is effectively *structuring your time*—your most important asset. You've got to devote enough of it to your work so that you can earn a living and enough of it to your non-working activities so that you can enjoy your life. Performance-Driven Thinkers integrate life and work, but work does not take up all their life.

The Roper Poll, the Harris Poll, the Gallup Poll, and the Universities of Maryland and Pennsylvania conduct studies yearly to see what Americans cherish the most. It wasn't until 1988 that Americans finally came to their senses—and put time as the number one item on the list. Time has been number one every year since 1989 and will remain number one for the rest of our lives. It's astonishing that it took so long for us to place time in its proper perspective, but better late than never. At least Performance-Driven Thinkers of the twenty-first century and beyond know that time is decidedly not money and that it is a finite asset not to be squandered.

A nationwide study conducted by *Adweek* magazine attempted to learn whether people would rather have free time or more money. Not surprisingly, 53 percent of the respondents said that they wanted free time. Among men, the choice of free time was made by 58 percent. Among people of ages 25 to 34, 61 percent selected free time. Among those 45 to 55, time was chosen by 56 percent.

A recent Gallup Poll revealed that the majority of Americans would rather work four days each week than five. Back in 1971, Americans actually preferred a five-day week. Slowly but surely, time is gaining stature.

## Everyone Will Know It

Just as data is the currency of the twenty-first century, time will be its most precious resource, *and everyone will know it*—you, your employees, your customers, your family. The more you can save time for these people, the more beloved a citizen of earth you will become. They will use the time you save them, according to one recent study, to be with their families, to travel, to study more, to compete at sports, and just to take it easy.

Ranked according to what people would do with their time, we learn that

- 15 percent would spend more time with their families

- 11 percent would relax

- 9 percent would travel

- 6 percent would spend time with their hobbies

- 6 percent would work around the house or garden

- 6 percent would go back to school or study more

- 5 percent would work more

- 5 percent would hunt, fish, play golf or tennis, or camp out

- 1 percent would read more

## The Benefits of Saving Time for People

Reverence for time is growing rapidly, and Performance-Driven Thinker–run companies must be prepared to honor it. Business strategies that save time for people help companies grow three times faster and profit *five times more* than companies with strategies that ignore this crucial need for speed. Companies that were aware of time overran their markets, stole the best customers, increased the loyalty of the customers they already had, and became the leading industry innovators. Better still, their success all but closed off the business to its competition. At best, only one or two competitors, moving as rapidly as they could, were able to stay in the game. The rest? Doomed.

To structure your business as the Performance-Driven Thinker would, begin by making a list of the tasks that must be accomplished in order for you to score bull's eyes on your targets. Some of these tasks may be handled by you, if no one can do them better. Others must be delegated. Some are a pure joy for you to undertake. Others are pure pain. Structure your time so that you do the work that you do best and that excites you most. Allow others to do the rest. Someone will love to complete tasks that you find distasteful. No task must be ignored. No goal must be unattended to. Fitting yourself into the picture in the best possible way requires talent. You want your business to succeed, and yet you want to sacrifice none of your goals, one of which is enjoying life while you work and enjoying work while you live.

## Efficiency vs. Effectiveness

Before we investigate sane and intelligent ways for you to structure your time, let's clarify the distinction between efficiency, which is good, and effectiveness, which is very good. Efficient people are excellent at saving time, but shortsightedness often causes their efficiency to get in the way of their effectiveness. If someone was to pack a parachute for you and brag about how they were so efficient that it took them only ten seconds, you'd be leery about jumping from the airplane for fear that their effectiveness took a back seat to their efficiency.

But if someone told you that they packed parachutes so effectively that not one has ever failed to open, you'd be a bit more confident wearing it during your plunge from the skies. You wouldn't give a hoot about efficiency and how rapidly the parachute was packed; so it should be for your Performance-Driven Enterprise. Run it efficiently to be sure, but never let efficiency get in the way of developing momentum that carries you toward your goals.

Effectiveness will carry you in the right direction. When structuring your time, remember that even though speed is a positive attribute, avoid it if it gets in the way of your overall effectiveness. Structure your time in order to accomplish the tasks that keep you on track, not whatever gets you down that track the fastest.

## Zen and the Art of Being Performance Driven

The Performance-Driven Thinker, although fascinated with ways of improving efficiency, is a real stickler about improving effectiveness and continually looks for methods of honing it. In *Zen and the Art of Motorcycle Maintenance*, the author Robert Pirsig was constantly working on his motorcycle—a labor of love—so that it never needed repairs. His mind was focused on the effectiveness of his machine and the pure enjoyment of working to improve it. If you consistently work on adding to the effectiveness of your earning endeavor, and if it is a labor of love, it will need few repairs.

When structuring your time, keep in the forefront of your mind that the previously mentioned Gallup poll showed that nearly eight in ten adult Americans feel that time is moving too fast for them. Six of ten say they enjoy non-working time the most, though 18 percent say they prefer being at work. More than five in ten bemoan the fact that they do not have the time to do the things that they really want to do. If you're to be the Performance-Driven Thinker I want you to be, you will be one of the two in ten Americans who feel that time is moving at a pace ideal for them. You'll be one of the five in ten Americans who have the time to do everything they want to do. It won't happen by accident. And it won't happen because of luck.

It will happen because you structured your time to give yourself time. True, your business needs a lot of your time. But it does not need all of your time. The only entity that needs *all* of your time is you. Give generously of that time to your business, but don't be too lavish. Leave enough for yourself. When you structure your time properly, you will have the time that you need and the time that your *business* needs. You will never sacrifice company profitability to get extra time. That extra time will be built into your existence.

Where do you begin when structuring your time? A good, but not very obvious, place is *yourself* and your own style. Although research into sleep and wakefulness continues at an increasing pace, we still have much to learn. But we do know that some people operate best starting early in the morning and then slow down in the early evening, whereas others are just getting started in the early evening. Darkness is when they are at their brightest.

## Tock-Tick, Tock-Tick

It's difficult to lead a life of going against your natural grain, forcing your body clock to say, tock-tick, tock-tick—so that if you hate getting up in the morning, you ought to sleep late and capitalize in your natural energy in the late afternoon. If your business requires a morning presence and you love sleeping until noon, you may have to delegate your duties to someone else during that time. If it requires someone to be around at night and you're in dreamland at dusk, let someone else run your show—or be clear on the times you will be on hand.

My clients and associates know never to call me early in the morning, because I'll be sleeping or reading the paper. They know never to call me on Fridays, because I'll be away hiking, skiing, or exploring in my Range Rover. They know I never answer the phone during the evenings, and they're aware that the worst times of all for calling me are Monday, Tuesday, Wednesday, and Thursday afternoons when I'm hardest at work, so they contact me at the times that fall in between the cracks. They keep conversations brief and they make intelligent use of my calendar and e-mail, especially e-mail, eliminating the necessity for much face-to-face contact. I have nothing against face-to-face contact, but I have a strong leaning towards inner fulfillment.

Performance-Driven Thinkers structure their time according to their priorities. They do not think in terms of nine to five, but instead in terms of accomplishing goals.

## Structure Your Time around Yourself

Performance-Driven Thinkers know when and how they function best and then arrange their schedule so that they can make their optimum contributions when they are at their peak. They know the importance of energy, vitality, and enthusiasm, and they know they will shortchange their work if they produce the most when they have the least to give. Their entire business plan is designed for *enlightened selfishness.* Peak performance is the result.

## Structure Your Time around Your Goals

Now that you've accommodated your strengths and style in structuring your business, you can devote attention to your skills as an entrepreneur. Match the operations of your business to your goals as closely as you can. You have honestly clarified your goals. You have been realistic. Structure your time to help you achieve those goals in the most effective manner possible. The way the things used to be done may not be the way they should be done now. Focus on attaining all your objectives.

## Structure Your Time around Your Family or Friends—or Both

Your kids growing up is a one-time performance. There are no encores. The good old days are happening now, and they include a lot more than your financial survival. Youth isn't wasted on the young when the young have their priorities on straight and refuse to allow their earning-a-living time to interfere with their living time. Business schools don't encourage entrepreneurs to structure their time to include family and friends, but they will in time. Why should you learn this lesson the hard way?

## Structure Your Time around Your Profits

Almost certainly, pursuit of the good old dollar bill will be one of your goals, so when you structure your limited time in this universe, be sure to direct the goodly portion of it towards amassing profits. Those profits may not come instantly, but when you do begin to generate them, they should increase in size every month if you're going about things right. That means you're getting wiser every month and learning from mistakes every month and that your time is well planned. The reality of dealing with people in different time zones, nationally and globally, makes an impact on how you will structure your time. Yet, it is possible to have time for yourself, your goals, your friends and family, and still turn a steadily increasing profit. One way is with delegating. The other is with technology.

## Structure Your Time with Technology

In the not-very-distant past, the best timesaver we had was a good grasp of time management—planning, making lists, prioritizing. That still is an ally of the Performance-Driven Thinker, but powerful new forces have joined the battle for time—your time—and the most potent is technology.

Technology has presented to time-conscious entrepreneurs a glorious selection of timesavers—computers, e-mail, fax machines, answering devices, pagers, websites, car phones, earphones, hands-free phones, even microwaves and books on tape. By incorporating this technology into your business modus operandi, along with the art of delegating, you will be able to structure your time in this evolved way.

Are there really people who can be successful entrepreneurs while avoiding the traps of workaholism and early burnout? Yes, they already exist. Do these people actually succeed while structuring their time according to the guidelines in this chapter? Yes, and success comes to them even more easily, because of how they have eliminated unnecessary stress from their lives.

More of these people succeed now than ever before in history. There will be more of them in the next ten years than there are now. These suggestions for structuring your time sound impractical for today's world, but much of today's world is yesterday's world. These suggestions are for tomorrow's world, guideposts that mark the Performance-Driven Thinker's way.

Entrepreneurs playing by the rules of the past run the risk of dying with regrets for things that they have not tried. While my mentor, friend, and co-author Jay Conrad Levinson lived in England, he had a friend who was a Catholic priest, eighty-one years old. One day he said that the thing that surprised him most about his calling was something he had learned while taking the final confession of people about to die. He said that none of them ever expressed regrets for things that they had done. They only regretted things that they *hadn't* done.

He said that he didn't want to die with any of those regrets. He lived his life so that he didn't. Now that you are aware of the land of the possible, I hope that you don't leave this world regretting that you didn't try your skill by walking the Performance-Driven Thinker's trail.

The ten ways we have shared with you to help sustain Performance-Driven Thinking, coupled with this deeper understanding of time management, will serve as a cornerstone for achieving new goals and accomplishments in your personal and professional life. Applying these will allow you to take Performance-Driven Thinking from the pages of this book and apply it to your daily lives. In striving for your best performance, you must realize that while you might not reach your overall goal today, you will certainly be able to appreciate the strides you are making through Performance-Driven Thinking.

Remember the following additional keys to successful long-term performance:

1. Come to play, not to watch.

2. Come to give, not to take.

3. Come to respect, not to disrespect.

4. Come to make a difference, not to waste time.

5. Come to win, not to lose.

"Don't measure yourself by what you have accomplished; measure yourself by what you should have accomplished with your ability."

**John Wooden**

# Chapter 10:

## Selecting Your Stage to Perform

While much of what we have written up to this point is about applying Performance-Driven Thinking, a major question that still remains is, where do I begin in this process? A good way to begin deploying Performance-Driven Thinking in your life is to answer the following five questions:

## 1. What is your passion?

Most likely the easiest place to begin your journey to performance is to determine your passion. Is it improving your health, making a higher income, or getting a higher-level position at work? Whether you make a choice to employ Performance-Driven Thinking in your personal or professional life, you have a greater opportunity for success when you discover once and for all what you are passionate about. Performance without passion is like a vehicle without fuel. Where your passion is, your time and energy eventually will be.

## 2. What challenges you?

Whenever we are called to perform in our lives, we want to use our best energy in an area where we find challenging. Many people today do not feel fulfilled because they are in relationships or jobs that are neither challenging nor rewarding. Most of the job-related surveys that have come out in the last decade clearly indicate that people perform the best and are the most dedicated to positions they find challenging. When we go through life without challenges, it is too easy to go through the motions. Challenges are what call us to a higher level of performance. If your stage is too easy, then your performance will suffer.

## 3. What stretches you?

After you have devoted time to identifying what you are extremely passionate about and what challenges you, the next step is to identify a performance stage that stretches your knowledge, skills, and abilities. Many of us may be able to overcome certain challenges within our lives without significant effort. Not everything that challenges us actually stretches us and causes us to grow. By selecting a performance stage that stretches you, you can improve your performance even beyond your challenges. Top performers love to grow their capabilities when pursuing their goals. We have all heard it said that anything in life worth having is worth working for. Performance-Driven Thinking clearly serves as a defining process of this thought.

## 4. Where is your support system?

Whenever performance is either required or demanded, it becomes essential for us to identify our individual support systems to reach our overall goal. Once you have identified a specific goal that will require a significant level of performance within your life, you must then be able to identify those around you who will be supportive in cheering you on toward that goal. Who will be that person at the finish line of your first 5K? Who will be there to applaud you when you finally graduate from college? Who will help you celebrate when you finally lose that weight you have been trying to lose for months? A stage without supporters makes for an empty performance. Imagine what it would be like if you had worked hard as a music performer to prepare for a concert for months, only to walk out and find an empty arena. Choosing the right stage to perform means finding positive supporters along the way. Who will support you when you take your stage to perform?

## 5. What are you willing to risk?

Every performance and challenge we face in life brings a certain level of risk. When we apply Performance-Driven Thinking to certain areas of our lives, we must understand that it could possibly lead to a life-changing attitude or event. As we decide to completely commit to pursuing performance, we must be willing to accept the risk that our success will bring. However, we can't forget to assess the risks from all angles. In addition to identifying the risks that pursuing performance may cause, perhaps the more important question we should ask ourselves is, If I do *not* pursue performance in my life, what will I be risking? Remember, we all have specific desires in our own lives, and only we can determine the level of risk we are willing to take to accomplish what we want, as well as the risk of not achieving it.

# The Path to the Work You Love: Twenty Characteristics of the Performance-Driven Thinker

As we said at the very beginning of the book, the goal of the Performance-Driven Thinker is the journey itself.

When the journey is the goal, you can begin with work that satisfies you. Time to spend enjoying activities other than the work you love and a remarkable freedom from work-related stress. Performance-Driven Thinkers, many of whom exist today well ahead of their time, have twenty characteristics in common. These twenty hallmarks fuel the commitment these entrepreneurs have—to themselves, their families, their communities, and their work.

Performance-Driven Thinkers set their sights on attaining these goals—as they live their dream of enjoying life and performing at their highest level, always creating win-win-win situations. You may remember some of these goals from previous chapters. If you're not sure what your life's work or passion is yet, let these twenty signposts guide your way. They will surely lead you to the performance of a lifetime.

**1. The Performance-Driven Thinker knows that the journey is the goal.** He also realizes that he is in control of his enterprise, not the other way around, and if he is dissatisfied with his journey, he is missing the point of the journey itself. Unlike old-fashioned enterprises, which often required gigantic sacrifices for the sake of the goal, *Performance-Driven Enterprises* place the goal of a pleasant journey ahead of the mere notion of sacrifices.

**2. The Performance-Driven Thinker achieves balance from the very start.** He builds free time into his work schedule so that balance is part of his enterprise. He respects his leisure time as much as his work time, never allowing too much of one to interfere with the other. Traditional entrepreneurs always placed work ahead of leisure and showed no respect for their own personal freedom. Performance-Driven Thinkers cherish their freedom as much as their work.

**3. The Performance-Driven Thinker is not in a hurry.** Unnecessary speed frequently undermines even the best-conceived strategies. Haste makes waste and sacrifices quality. The Performance-Driven Thinker is fully aware that patience is his ally and he has planned intelligently to eliminate most emergencies that call for moving fast. His pace is always steady, but never rushed.

**4. The Performance-Driven Thinker uses stress as a benchmark.** If he feels any stress, he knows he must be going about things in the wrong way. Performance-Driven Thinkers do not accept stress as a part of doing business and recognize any stress as a warning sign that something's the matter—in the work plan of the Performance-Driven Thinker or in the business itself, adjustments are made to eliminate the cause of the stress, which causes the stress to disappear.

**5. The Performance-Driven Thinker looks forward to work.**
He has a love affair with his work and considers himself blessed to be paid for doing the work that he does. He is good at his work, energizing his passion for it in a quest to learn more about it and improve his understanding of it, thereby increasing his skills. The Performance-Driven Thinker doesn't think about his retirement, for he would never want to stop doing the work he loves.

**6. The Performance-Driven Thinker has no weaknesses.**
He is effective in every aspect of his enterprise, because he has filled in the gaps between his strengths and talents with people who abound at the prowess he lacks. He is very much a team player and allies himself with other Performance-Driven Thinkers who share the team spirit and possess complementary skills. He values his teammates as much as old-fashioned entrepreneurs valued their independence.

**7. The Performance-Driven Thinker is fusion oriented.**
He is always on the alert to fuse his business with other synergistic enterprises in town, in America, in the world. He is willing to combine marketing efforts, production skills, information, leads, mailing lists, and anything else to increase his effectiveness and marketing reach while reducing the cost of achieving those goals. His fusion efforts are intentionally short term and rarely permanent. In his business relationships, instead of thinking "marriage," he thinks "fling."

**8. The Performance-Driven Thinker does not kid himself.**
He knows that if he overestimates his own abilities, he

runs the risk of skimping on the quality he represents to his customers, employees, investors, suppliers, and fusion partners. He forces himself to face reality on a daily basis and realizes that all of his business practices must always be evaluated in the glaring light of what is really happening, instead of what should be happening.

**9. The Performance-Driven Thinker lives in the present.** He is well aware of the past, very enticed by the future, but the here and now is where he resides, embracing the technologies of the present, leaving future technologies on the horizon right where they belong, until late when they are ripe and ready. He is alert to the new, wary of the avant-garde, and wooed from the old only by improvement, not mere change.

**10. A Performance-Driven Thinker understands the precious nature of time.** He doesn't buy into that old lie that "time is money" and knows in his heart that time is far more important than money. He knows that time is life. He is aware that his customers and prospects feel the same way about time, so he respects theirs and wouldn't dare waste it. As a practicing Performance-Driven Thinker, he is the epitome of efficiency, but never lets it interfere with his effectiveness.

**11. The Performance-Driven Thinker always operates according to a plan.** He knows who he is, where is he going, and how he will get there. He knows why he is here in the first place. He is prepared, knows that anything can and will happen, and can deal with the barriers to entrepreneurial success, because his plan has foreseen them and shown exactly how to surmount them. The Performance-Driven Thinker reevaluates his plan regularly and does not hesitate to make changes in it, though commitment to the plan is part of his very being.

**12. The Performance-Driven Thinker is flexible.** He is guided by a strategy for success and knows the difference between a guide and a master. When it is necessary, the Performance-Driven Thinker changes, accepting change is part of the status quo, not ignoring or battling it. He is able to adapt to new situations, realizes that service is whatever his customers want it to be, and knows that inflexible things become brittle and break.

**13. The Performance-Driven Thinker aims for results more than growth.** He is focused on profitability and balance, vitality and improvement, value and quality, more than size and growth. His plan calls for steadily increasing profits without the sacrifice of personal time, so his actions are oriented to hitting those targets instead of growing for the sake of growth alone. He is wary of becoming large and does not equate hugeness with excellence.

**14. The Performance-Driven Thinker is dependent upon many people.** He knows that the age of the lone-wolf entrepreneur—independent and proud of it—has passed. The Performance-Driven Thinker is very dependent upon his fusion business partners, his employees, his customers, his suppliers, and his mentors. He got where he is with his own wings, his own determination, his own smarts, and as a Performance-Driven Thinker, with a little help from a lot of friends.

**15. The Performance-Driven Thinker is constantly learning.** A seagull flies in circles in the sky looking for food in an endless quest. When it finally finds the food, the seagull lands and eats its fill. When it has completed the meal then returns to the sky, only to fly in circles again searching for food although it has eaten. Humans have only one comparable instinct, the need for constant learning. Performance-Driven Thinkers have this need in spades.

**16. The Performance-Driven Thinker is passionate about work.** His enthusiasm for what he does is apparent to everyone who sees his work. This enthusiasm spreads to everyone who works with him, even to his customers. In its purest form, this enthusiasm is best expressed as the word *passion*—an intense feeling that burns within him and is manifested in the devotion he demonstrates towards his business.

**17. The Performance-Driven Thinker is focused on the goal.** He knows that balance does not come easily and that he must rid himself of the values and expectations of his ancestors. To do this, he must remain focused on his journey, seeing the future clearly while concentrating on the present. He is aware that the minutia of life and business can distract him, so he does what is necessary to make those distractions only momentary.

**18. The Performance-Driven Thinker is disciplined about the tasks at hand.** He is keenly aware that every time he writes a task on his daily calendar he is making a promise to himself. As a Performance-Driven Thinker who does not cater to himself, he keeps those promises, knowing that the achievement of his goals will be more than an adequate reward for his discipline. He finds it easy to be disciplined, because of the payback offered by the leisure that follows.

**19. The Performance-Driven Thinker is well organized at home and at work.** He does not waste valuable time looking for items that have been misplaced and stays organized as he works and as new work comes to him. His astute sense of order is fueled by the efficiency that results from it. He shares his ability to organize with those who work with him. Yet, the Performance-Driven Thinker never squanders precious time by becoming over organized.

**20. The Performance-Driven Thinker has an upbeat attitude.** Because he knows that life is unfair, that problems arise, that to err is human, and that the cool shall inherit the earth, he manages to take obstacles in stride, keeping his perspective and his sense of humor. His ever-present optimism is grounded in his ability to perceive the positive side of things—recognizing the negative but never dwelling on it, his positive attitude is contagious and spreads rapidly.

Perhaps in the light of these twenty criteria you're thinking, "Do Performance-Driven Thinkers exist in real life or only in fairy tales?" The answer is yes. They do exist in real life, but their success and balance are like a fairy tale. They exist all around you, in every state of the union, in every nation on Earth, in every ethnic minority, in all age groups in both genders.

Armed with the right vision and the right information, Performance-Driven Thinkers can attain heights never envisioned by their parents. They can add the element of love to their work, for they will devote themselves only to work that they love.

Kahlil Gibran in *The Prophet* said that "work is love made visible, and if you cannot work with love, but only with distaste, it is better that you should leave your work and sit at the gate of the temple, and take alms of those who work with joy." Spoken like a true Performance-Driven Thinker.

Selecting the stage to start your performance is an individual decision. We have tried to share a thought process and practical guidelines that will allow you to step up to your stage of choice in your personal or professional life. Just think about it: if each one of us were to get up each morning and live out our day doing what we are passionate about, what challenges us, and what stretches us, while at the same time having the support of our friends and loved ones, what a valued life we all would live.

**"The Performance-Driven Thinker knows that the journey is the goal."**

**David Hancock**

# CHAPTER 11:

# The Moment of Truth:

*Performers Win; Bystanders Wait*

During this journey toward Performance-Driven Thinking, we have examined a number of issues that could prevent performance within your personal or professional life. But it all boils down to whether you will choose to step up to the plate or remain in the dugout of life. In chapter 1, we challenged you to embrace the fact that you were born to perform. Now that you have examined the road to Performance-Driven Thinking, the choice is yours: will you be a performer in life, or a bystander?

Performers:

- Are self-starters

- Have self-discipline

- Are self-guided

- Are detail-oriented

- Assume responsibility

- Are self-learners

- Think positive

- Are coachable

- Are task-oriented

- Are self-rewarded

Bystanders:

- Lack initiative

- Resist feedback

- Require guidance

- Escape detail

- Lack responsibility

- Easily distracted

- Are quick to blame

- Seek rewards

- Procrastinate

- Lack self-confidence

## Am I A Performer or a Bystander?

Now we have come to the moment of truth: are you a performer or a bystander? To help you answer this question, we have developed the following questionnaire.

For the following questions, select True or False.

1. I have a great deal of self-initiative. True or False

2. I am usually the first one to start or complete a specific task or goal. True or False

3. I constantly pay attention to the performance of those around me. True or False

4. I get frustrated easily when others oppose my way of doing things. True or False

5. I generally do not let the performance or lack of performance impact my activity. True or False

6. In order for me to perform at my top level, I need personal or professional recognition. True or False

7.  I am not concerned when a task is left incomplete. True or False

8.  The impact of my personal or professional performance is not a major concern of mine. True or False

9.  The success of my day is not a direct result of my performance. True or False

10. I do not have an issue with allowing those around me to outperform me. True or False

## Scoring

**The following answers indicate you are on the path toward Performance-Driven Thinking:**

1.  True

2.  True

3.  True

4.  False

5.  False

6.  False

7.  False

8. False

9. False

10. False

## If You Are a Bystander

If, after the quiz above, you have determined that you are a performer, congratulations! If you have realized you are a bystander, don't worry. The best way forward is to know where you're starting. The remainder of the chapter will help you discover what's holding you back, and what can move you forward.

So far in this book, you have identified your opponents to performance, your fears and risk factors regarding performance, and your knowledge, skills, and abilities. What do you think is holding you back from performance? Is it your fear of failure? Is it your comfortable lifestyle? Is it a perceived lack of support? Each one of us has the same number of hours and minutes in a day that make our lives count. And while those around you may support the efforts in a number of ways, your decision to move forward depends first upon your individual desire and will to perform.

Many of us know loving, caring parents who have provided a tremendous amount of moral and financial assistance to guide their children down the pathway of success. Many of us could cite personal stories about the parents and grandparents who gave everything to help their children become successful. However, too often these stories have an unhappy ending: even though these children and grandchildren had their stage set to become an instant success, many of them simply did not have the will and desire to perform.

So why do some people simply practice the game of life, watching opportunities come right down the plate in life and pass them by, while others readily step up to the plate and take a swing? Beyond what we have already mentioned in previous chapters, there are several other issues we all face. The following key factors tend to encourage people to be bystanders in a world that needs their performance. See if you can identify any in yourself.

**Procrastination:** One of the biggest reasons why people will not step up and perform is the belief that our actions can wait until another time or place. The art of procrastination is alive and well in our society. Many individuals will not perform today what they think can wait until tomorrow. This translates into an issue of personal time management. While the clock is slowly ticking every day, we all have to admit that there are times when we could be performing, yet we remain idle. Instead of labeling procrastination as a waste of our time, we should ask ourselves, what is the best use of our time? Every day we are given a certain amount of time and energy to accomplish our personal and professional goals. When we fail to engage our efforts, we have actually allowed our time and energy to be non-productive. While no one expects anyone to be at a high level of performance all hours of the day or night, we should learn to expect a basic level of accomplishment from ourselves every day, both personally and professionally.

**The-Someone-Else-Will-Do-It Syndrome:** When is the last time you contacted a business or organization and got passed around to a number of different branches or offices in their attempt to get something accomplished? It is amazing how many people in today's society will quickly pass the buck, even in their areas of responsibilities. It is so easy to sit back as a bystander and to force others into performance while we watch from the back seat. But falling prey to the Someone-Else-Will-Do-It Syndrome is self-defeating in the long run. When you always allow others to take the lead in your personal or professional responsibilities becomes a consistent easy hiding place. Remember, you were born to perform! Performance can only become a reality in our lives when we step up and face our personal responsibility to perform. Our performance ultimately cannot be measured by what others are producing, but by our personal achievement.

**The No-One-Will-Notice Syndrome:** People in our society tend to think that if they slack off in their personal and professional performance, no one will notice. The problem with the No-One-Will-Notice Syndrome is the same as the Someone-Else-Will-Do-It Syndrome: it hijacks our personal responsibility. When we start to think that no one will notice, we slack off in our efforts even further. Our first mistake is not having the self-discipline to care that our own efforts are falling short, even if no one else notices. Performance-Driven Thinking has to be a personal choice. If we are honest, somewhere deep down we will realize when our performance level is cheating ourselves and others around us. Yes, you may have escaped the limelight of performance by thinking others did not notice. While disguising your abilities may fool others, the question is, at the end of the day, how do you feel about your efforts? A conscious lack of performance not only hijacks your own personal responsibility, but also negatively impacts those around you.

# Shifting from Bystander to Performer

The process of Performance-Driven Thinking goes much deeper than theory. It depends on action. At times we can overthink and research ourselves to death. That's why we embrace the fundamental principle that "faith without works is dead!" So if you find yourself stuck in bystander mode, here are three basic action steps you can take to get you moving toward performance:

**Know your role:** We should go into every situation knowing what is expected of us. You cannot perform a goal you don't understand or even know about. Once we know what is expected of us, we can begin to actively work on our limitations. This will lead us not only to meet but to exceed the expectations that have been placed on us, and this will add up to true performance. If a true performer is going to succeed, they first establish their position in the game. Imagine a football team where every player thought it was their role to be the quarterback. Imagine a business where everyone is trying to be the chief executive officer. Imagine your home where there is no pecking order and parents never take charge. Each of us needs to know, whether in our personal or professional lives, what is our role regarding performance in this area? If there is any doubt, ask the question.

**Accept your role:** One issue that can prevent performance and block progress is when we have difficulty accepting our individual role in a larger process. This goes beyond the key issue of knowing your job. After you answer the question, "What is my role?" you need to ask yourself, "Can I accept that role?" Certainly each of us has experienced situations when someone in our organization has tried to perform a role that was not theirs. Not only is it essential for you to know what you are expected to accomplish, it is very important that you accept it. On the other hand, never feel that you should accept a role that was not intended for you. When we attempt to operate outside of our expected roles, we tend to minimize our overall impact in the process. In order for us to be successful, all participants in the process should have a clearly identified role on that road to success. When we become comfortable with accepting exactly what our individual responsibilities will be, we become better, more efficient performers.

**Play your role:** Beyond knowing and accepting your individual role, performance requires you to actively play your role. Many people have the knowledge, skills and abilities to perform certain tasks. But we all know of situations when people were supposed to carry out specific roles but never actually performed their tasks. For whatever reason, you may feel hesitant in carrying out your part of the process. But all of the personal and job-related training that you have as a person is only as good as your ability to put action to that preparation. Remember, you don't have to be perfect—your abilities will improve as you use them.

# Performance-Driven Thinking Personality Traits

Performance-Driven Thinkers are both born and made. If they lack these traits, they work to develop them.

Working with the some of the smartest minds in business today, I have noticed eight personality traits these Performance-Driven Thinkers possess. And try as I may, I simply have not found an exception to this observation. Performance-Driven Thinkers have every one of these eight characteristics.

I hope that you already have all eight of these personality traits, or that you can at least develop the one or two that may be lacking. Let's examine the eight right here and right now.

**1. Patience:** I start with this trait because it's the most important by far. A study was conducted to see how many times you must penetrate a person's mind with your selling proposition before you convert that person from a state of total apathy to a state of purchase readiness. Amazingly, the researchers came up with an answer. It was nine. Your message must penetrate a mind nine times before that person will buy what you are selling. And that's the good news. The bad news is that for every three times you put out the word, your prospects are paying attention only two times.

So you market by advertising, e-mailing, telemarketing, signs, direct mail, anything—you put the word out three times, and it penetrates your prospect's mind one time. What do you suppose happens? Nothing happens. Zilch. Okay, you put the word out six times, entering the mind of your prospect two times. What happens then?

Again, not one thing happens. All right, now you put the word out nine times, and you have penetrated the mind of your prospect three times. What happens?

Your prospect knows he or she has heard of you before. That's what happens. No sale. No cigar. Not yet, at least.

Sticking with the drill, you put the word out twelve times, and your prospect's mind has been pierced four times. What happens then? What happens is that your prospect realizes he or she has seen your marketing before, and people figure that if they keep seeing your marketing, you must be doing something right. But still, nobody is buying anything.

Now, you put out the word fifteen times and penetrate your prospect's mind five times. At this point, the prospect probably reads every word of your ad or letter, probably even goes online to see what you've been offering all along. At this point, most small advertisers figure they've been doing everything wrong, and so they abandon their marketing program. DON'T DO IT! NOT YET! This horrid state of affairs is called *sellus interruptus. The sale is never consummated because the marketing chief didn't have the patience to hang in there.*

After you've put the word out eighteen times, and you've penetrated a mind six times, the person begins to consider when they'll make the purchase. Put out the word twenty-one times, and you've penetrated a mind seven times. The person begins to think about where they'll get the money, how they'll pay for it. Put the word out twenty-four times, and the prospects, with their minds penetrated eight times, write in their calendar when they will buy from you. They check with whomever they must check with before making a purchase. Finally, you get the word out twenty-seven times, penetrate your prospects' minds nine times, and they buy from you. Eventually, the profits come rolling in.

Think that process can take place if you have no patience? *No way.* That's why patience remains the most important of the eight personality characteristics.

**2. Imagination:** This doesn't necessarily refer to headlines or graphics or jingles or being clever as much as it does facing up to reality. If you're going to do a direct mailing, face up to the fact that everyone and their cousin does direct mailings. Why should your envelope get opened?

Because you've got the imagination to pop for first-class postage and to put eleven stamps on your envelope: two 6-centers, four 4-centers, two 3-centers, and six 2-centers. Who could resist opening an envelope with fourteen stamps? Not only will it be opened, but it will be opened first. Doesn't take a lot of money; does take a powerful imagination.

**3. Sensitivity:** People who run first-rate marketing shows are sensitive to their market, their prospects, the economy, the community, and the competition. It's a key personality trait.

**4. Ego strength:** The first people who will tire of your marketing program will be your co-workers, followed closely by your employees, your family, and your friends. They will counsel you to change because they are bored. Your prospects are not bored and have barely heard of you. Your customers will not be bored and will forever read your marketing materials to justify the fact that they still do business with you.

**5. Aggressiveness:** You need to be aggressive in your spending and your thinking. When you hear that the average US business invests 4 percent of gross revenues in marketing, you want to invest 6 to 10 percent. When you hear there are 200 marketing weapons, you want to use at least half of them.

**6. Constant learning:** A seagull flies in endless circles, seeking food. When it finds food, it eats its fill and then flies in circles again, looking for more food. Seagulls just have to look for food. Humans have one instinct that is just as strong. Know what it is? To learn. Performance-Driven Thinkers know a lot but keep learning more.

**7. Generosity:** Performance-Driven Thinkers view marketing as an opportunity to help their prospects and customers succeed at their goals, whatever they may be. They think of things they can give away to help those people. They are generous with their time and their information.

**8. Action oriented:** Many people read books, hear CDs, take courses, and attend seminars. But most of them keep this information within them. Performance-Driven Thinkers learn the very same ways, but they take action based upon what they have learned. They know that action is the power behind Performance-Driven Thinking.

Those are the eight and the only eight traits that great Performance-Driven Thinkers seem to have in common. I sure hope all eight words apply to you.

Benjamin Franklin said that the three hardest things in the world are diamonds, steel, and knowing yourself. Compare the eight Performance-Driven Thinking personality traits with your own, and then be honest in knowing which ones you must develop even more.

In the list below, put a checkmark next to each of the Performance-Driven Thinking personality characteristics you possess. The character traits you currently have are:

❏ Patience

❏ Imagination

❏ Sensitivity

❏ Ego strength

❏ Aggressiveness

- ❑ Constant learning

- ❑ Generosity

- ❑ Being action oriented

## Action Steps

**Circle each personality trait that does not have a checkmark.**

Begin developing those traits in yourself.

Put a checkmark next to each trait you are able to develop. The goal is to have a checkmark next to each trait.

Performance is not about sitting on the sidelines of life and work. Performance is about playing our roles to the best of our abilities and always looking to improve our performance. The old phrase "action speaks louder than words" truly defines Performance-Driven Thinking.

**"The only thing procrastination and performance have in common is the first letter."**

**Bobby Kipper**

# Conclusion:

## The Stage Is Set—Now Introducing You

If we had been producing a movie, at this point you would hear the famous words, "Lights, camera, action!" During our journey toward Performance-Driven Thinking, we have covered a great deal of territory in our effort to convince you that your individual performance in life is a *choice*. We started this journey with the simple idea that you were born to perform. To enhance your ability to perform, we encouraged you to consider that to win in life, status quo thinking has to be a thing of the past. We then made the process simple by introducing the definition of Performance-Driven Thinking, which is the thought process that connects the desire to perform with the will to perform.

We then explored how important Performance-Driven Thinking is in your personal life, specifically in your health, finances, and personal relationships. We then explored the idea of performance at work, and even embraced and promoted the idea of Performance-Driven Leadership. Finally, we shared with you various reasons why individuals find it easy not to perform—even providing a number of common excuses used every day. And throughout, we cast the vision of balance for Performance-Driven Thinking, emphasizing that the best performance occurs without stress, perfectionism, or workaholism. The journey is the goal!

We hope you have noticed there was nothing complex or complicated about Performance-Driven Thinking. While many people will view it as common sense, others will still find ways to escape the performance of a lifetime. So what about you? Where will you fall on the spectrum of performance? Will you simply read the chapters of this book and go on with a life accepting a destiny controlled by others? Or will you take the attitude of a new athlete or employee that has been recruited into a particular team or organization, intending to rise to the occasion and perform at a top level?

When considering our own thinking about performance, we are quickly reminded of various professional sports and their method of drafting players to individual teams. Each year sports players from all over the country work hard in hopes of earning the opportunity of a lifetime to play professional sports. These individuals did not become professional stars overnight. Every decision they have made in their personal and professional lives has been focused on helping them seize this opportunity. You don't win championships without developing, practicing, and advancing your skill level. This example may not resonate with those who are not involved in sports, but Performance-Driven Thinking and performance itself must no longer be reserved for the playing field.

To bring this closer to home as we end our journey, you must be convinced that the life you are living is much like a competitive playing field, and just like competitive athletes, your attitude toward performance will be the cornerstone of your success in your personal and professional life. The spectators in the stands are your family members, friends, and co-workers, who will be there to view your performance at home and at work. Your closest supporters are those whom you will hear cheer the loudest, but at the end of the day, when the applause is weak, performance still matters. At times in your life, you will feel like you are performing in an empty arena. You may not hear the roar of a crowd or the kind words of family or close friends on a daily basis, but remember that the stage is set, and the world is waiting to see your knowledge, skills, and abilities in action.

So why wait any longer? You control the lights on your stage. You control when the curtain goes up. You control when the performance of your life begins and ends. You are never too young or too old to embrace a level of performance. So the challenge is yours. Starting today, decide what you desire—and once and for all, go for the gold!

## FIVE STEPS TO PERFORMANCE-DRIVEN THINKING

1. Realize you were born to perform.

2. Your education and life experiences have prepared you to perform.

3. Your knowledge, skills, and abilities are your tools to perform.

4. Establish what you want with clear goals.

5. Take willful action to achieve it by joining other performers at www.performancedrivenacademy.com.

"The Performance-Driven Thinker lives in the present."

**David Hancock**

# Performance-Driven Academy

*Take your performance to the next level by becoming a member of our Performance-Driven Academy!*

Each month, we will explore **Performance-Driven Thinking** at a much deeper level through specialized classes, tutorials, and actionable lessons. Our goal is to help you achieve your best performance and have greater impact.

**Members Benefit With:**

- Weekly Exclusive Performance Tips
- Performance-Driven Coaching Videos
- Exclusive Audio Updates
- Live Q&A Sessions with the Authors
- Discounts to Performance-Driven Events

# Performance-Driven Mastermind

**www.PerformanceDrivenMastermind.com**

*Our Performance-Driven Masterminds are small one-day Elite Mastermind Meetings in our hometown area of Hampton Roads, Virginia.*

Here are the details:

- The masterminds will last ONE day, usually on a Wednesday from 8:30 AM to 5 PM.

- The location is at an exclusive, supremely cool location, in Hampton, Virginia. (Yes, REALLY!)

- The attendees are all super-achievers, or up-and-comers. Everyone brings something to the table worth learning or knowing.

- Everyone has the opportunity to bring a problem, question, or business challenge before the mastermind group. And get the answer, solution, or resource they need.

- There will be NO PITCHING, or selling of any kind permitted. Not even by me.

There are only a handful of seats available for each mastermind. 12, to be exact.

Register here. Do it now.

www.PerformanceDrivenMastermind.com

# ABOUT THE AUTHORS

**David Hancock** is the founder of Morgan James Publishing, chairman of Guerrilla Marketing International, and co-author of twelve books, including *The Best of Guerrilla Marketing* and *The Entrepreneurial Author*. NASDAQ cites David as one of the world's most prestigious business leaders, and he is reported to be the future of publishing. As founder of Morgan James Publishing, he was named a finalist in the Best Chairman category in The American Business Awards, hailed as "the business world's own Oscars" by the *New York Post*. David was also selected for *Fast Company* magazine's Fast 50 for his leadership, creative thinking, significant accomplishments, and significant impact on the industry over the next ten years.

David also serves as president of the executive board for Habitat for Humanity Peninsula and Greater Williamsburg, and chairman of the board of the National Center for the Prevention of Community Violence.

**Bobby Kipper** is a bestselling author, speaker, and coach, and the co-founder of Performance Driven Thinking™. He has spent over thirty years providing leadership development, training, and coaching to both the government and private sectors. Bobby believes that we were "born to perform," and his motivational style of speaking and coaching has taken thousands to their best performance to date. In addition, Bobby is the director of the National Center for the Prevention of Community Violence and is passionate about quality of life and human rights issues for all Americans. His programs to prevent and reduce violence have been featured by the White House, Congress, and thirty-five states across America.